AF771146

SUBCOMMITTEE ON THE CONSTITUTION

STEVE CHABOT, Ohio, *Chairman*

STEVE KING, Iowa
WILLIAM L. JENKINS, Tennessee
SPENCER BACHUS, Alabama
JOHN N. HOSTETTLER, Indiana
MELISSA A. HART, Pennsylvania
TOM FEENEY, Florida
J. RANDY FORBES, Virginia

JERROLD NADLER, New York
JOHN CONYERS, JR., Michigan
ROBERT C. SCOTT, Virginia
MELVIN L. WATT, North Carolina
ADAM B. SCHIFF, California

PAUL B. TAYLOR, *Chief Counsel*
E. STEWART JEFFRIES, *Counsel*
HILARY FUNK, *Counsel*
MINDY BARRY, *Full Committee Counsel*
DAVID LACHMANN, *Minority Professional Staff Member*

# PRIVACY AND CIVIL LIBERTIES IN THE HANDS OF THE GOVERNMENT POST-SEPTEMBER 11, 2001: RECOMMENDATIONS OF THE 9/11 COMMISSION AND THE U.S. DEPARTMENT OF DEFENSE TECHNOLOGY AND PRIVACY ADVISORY COMMITTEE

---

## JOINT HEARING

BEFORE THE

SUBCOMMITTEE ON
COMMERCIAL AND ADMINISTRATIVE LAW

AND THE

SUBCOMMITTEE ON THE CONSTITUTION

OF THE

COMMITTEE ON THE JUDICIARY
HOUSE OF REPRESENTATIVES

ONE HUNDRED EIGHTH CONGRESS

SECOND SESSION

---

AUGUST 20, 2004

---

**Serial No. 113**

---

Printed for the use of the Committee on the Judiciary

Available via the World Wide Web: http://www.house.gov/judiciary

U.S. GOVERNMENT PRINTING OFFICE

95–498 PDF WASHINGTON : 2005

For sale by the Superintendent of Documents, U.S. Government Printing Office
Internet: bookstore.gpo.gov Phone: toll free (866) 512–1800; DC area (202) 512–1800
Fax: (202) 512–2250 Mail: Stop SSOP, Washington, DC 20402–0001

## COMMITTEE ON THE JUDICIARY

F. JAMES SENSENBRENNER, JR., Wisconsin, *Chairman*

HENRY J. HYDE, Illinois
HOWARD COBLE, North Carolina
LAMAR SMITH, Texas
ELTON GALLEGLY, California
BOB GOODLATTE, Virginia
STEVE CHABOT, Ohio
WILLIAM L. JENKINS, Tennessee
CHRIS CANNON, Utah
SPENCER BACHUS, Alabama
JOHN N. HOSTETTLER, Indiana
MARK GREEN, Wisconsin
RIC KELLER, Florida
MELISSA A. HART, Pennsylvania
JEFF FLAKE, Arizona
MIKE PENCE, Indiana
J. RANDY FORBES, Virginia
STEVE KING, Iowa
JOHN R. CARTER, Texas
TOM FEENEY, Florida
MARSHA BLACKBURN, Tennessee

JOHN CONYERS, JR., Michigan
HOWARD L. BERMAN, California
RICK BOUCHER, Virginia
JERROLD NADLER, New York
ROBERT C. SCOTT, Virginia
MELVIN L. WATT, North Carolina
ZOE LOFGREN, California
SHEILA JACKSON LEE, Texas
MAXINE WATERS, California
MARTIN T. MEEHAN, Massachusetts
WILLIAM D. DELAHUNT, Massachusetts
ROBERT WEXLER, Florida
TAMMY BALDWIN, Wisconsin
ANTHONY D. WEINER, New York
ADAM B. SCHIFF, California
LINDA T. SÁNCHEZ, California

PHILIP G. KIKO, *Chief of Staff-General Counsel*
PERRY H. APELBAUM, *Minority Chief Counsel*

---

### SUBCOMMITTEE ON COMMERCIAL AND ADMINISTRATIVE LAW

CHRIS CANNON, Utah *Chairman*

HOWARD COBLE, North Carolina
JEFF FLAKE, Arizona
JOHN R. CARTER, Texas
MARSHA BLACKBURN, Tennessee
STEVE CHABOT, Ohio
TOM FEENEY, Florida

MELVIN L. WATT, North Carolina
JERROLD NADLER, New York
TAMMY BALDWIN, Wisconsin
WILLIAM D. DELAHUNT, Massachusetts
ANTHONY D. WEINER, New York

RAYMOND V. SMIETANKA, *Chief Counsel*
SUSAN A. JENSEN, *Counsel*
DIANE K. TAYLOR, *Counsel*
JAMES DALEY, *Full Committee Counsel*
STEPHANIE MOORE, *Minority Counsel*

# CONTENTS

AUGUST 20, 2004

OPENING STATEMENT



WITNESSES



APPENDIX

# PRIVACY AND CIVIL LIBERTIES IN THE HANDS OF THE GOVERNMENT POST-SEPTEMBER 11, 2001: RECOMMENDATIONS OF THE 9/11 COMMISSION AND THE U.S. DEPARTMENT OF DEFENSE TECHNOLOGY AND PRIVACY ADVISORY COMMITTEE

---

**FRIDAY, AUGUST 20, 2004**

House of Representatives,
Subcommittee on Commercial
and Administrative Law,
Committee on the Judiciary,
*Washington, DC.*

The Subcommittee met, pursuant to call, at 10:06 a.m., in Room 2141, Rayburn House Office Building, Hon. Chris Cannon [Chairman of the Subcommittee on Commercial and Administrative Law] presiding.

Mr. Cannon. The Subcommittee will come to order. I want to thank you all for joining us, especially our panel.

Today, before we formally start our proceedings, Chairman Chabot and I wanted to sincerely thank and recognize our colleagues on both Subcommittees and on both sides of the aisle for taking time out of their really busy schedules—for me, it was difficult, but I know that it was for everyone else—so as to attend the hearing this morning.

As many of you know, August is typically when Members of Congress return to their districts to catch up on constituent matters and spend time with their families. Wait a minute, do you guys have families? It is a time when we call it our home district work period. We want to thank everyone for coming out.

In these extraordinary times, we have to undertake extraordinary measures to deal with certain pressing issues. It also goes without saying that we express our sincere gratitude to our esteemed witnesses, each of whom reflects the greatest hallmarks of public service. We appreciate your contributions to our deliberations today.

The title of today's hearing, "Oversight Hearing on Privacy and Civil Liberties in the Hands of the Government Post-September 11, 2001: Recommendations of the 9/11 Commission and the U.S. Department of Defense Technology and Privacy Advisory Committee", which we will refer to as "TAPAC", clearly explains why we are here.

As many of you know, the 9/11 Commission filed its final report last month. What some of you may not know, however, is that the report includes several recommendations intended to protect our citizens' privacy and civil liberties. In addition, it recommends that the Federal Government set standards for the issuance of birth certificates and sources of identification such as driver's licenses to promote secure identification information.

While most media headlines have emphasized the Commission's antiterrorism proposals, I believe the privacy and civil liberties recommendations are among those most critical to our Nation's future and which will form part of the focus of our hearing.

Today's proceedings will also focus on certain recommendations the TAPAC Committee made regarding safeguarding informational privacy. By way of background, TAPAC was established by Secretary Rumsfeld as an independent, bipartisan committee to examine the privacy ramifications presented by data mining activities by the Defense Department. I think we all agree that Secretary Rumsfeld is to be commended for taking this initiative and for ensuring that TAPAC's membership included some of our Nation's most respected experts in the fields of constitutional and privacy law. I am informed that among the many luminaries who testified before TAPAC was our colleague from New York, Mr. Nadler. Thank you.

Advances in technology have increasingly facilitated the collection and dissemination of personally identifiable information, but have also correspondingly increased the potential for misuse of such information. As the recently renamed Government Accountability Office observed, these advances bring substantial Federal information benefits, as well as increasing responsibilities and concerns.

Interestingly, TAPAC over the course of its deliberations determined that as the Defense Department was not alone in its conduct of data mining activities, it was necessary for it to address this issue through a series of Government-wide recommendations. The purpose of today's hearing is to examine the validity of these recommendations and those of the 9/11 Commission that relate to privacy and civil liberties and to determine whether they warrant a legislative response.

We would especially appreciate any guidance from our witnesses about how the Congress, in crafting such legislation, can best protect our citizens' privacy without compromising legitimate law enforcement and terrorism detection efforts.

As our witnesses know, it has been 30 years since the Privacy Commission was established as part of the Privacy Act of 1974. I would be interested in having our witnesses comment on whether now is the time to reestablish a privacy commission that would specifically focus on Government privacy issues, especially given all the technological developments that have occurred since the Commission filed its final report in 1977 and the current state of our Nation's security concerns.

I should also note that both my Subcommittee, the Subcommittee on Commercial and Administrative Law, and Chairman Chabot's Subcommittee, the Constitution Subcommittee, have played a major role with respect to protecting personal privacy and civil liberties in this era of heightened security under the leadership and guidance of Mr. Sensenbrenner, the Chairman of the full Judiciary Committee.

As both the 9/11 Commission Report and the TAPAC concluded, it is no easy task to balance the competing goals of keeping our Nation secure and protecting the privacy rights of our Nation's citizens. I believe that our respective Subcommittees of the Judiciary Committee are uniquely and best suited to study and resolve these issues.

Our accomplishments, to date, include the establishment of the first statutorily-created privacy office in a Federal agency, namely the Department of Homeland Security. We have also spearheaded the creation of a similar office in the Justice Department, which is contained in the legislation now pending in the Senate. In addition, both my Subcommittee and the Constitution Subcommittee have considered and supported legislation requiring a Federal agency to prepare a privacy impact analysis for proposed and final rules, and to include this analysis in the notice of public comment issued in conjunction with the publication of such rules.

I will conclude my opening remarks with a quote from one of our Founding Fathers. As I think you will agree, Mr. Hamilton's observations and warnings—and here we are dealing with the earlier Mr. Hamilton—are as meaningful today as they were when he wrote them more than 200 years ago. "Safety from external danger is the most powerful director of national conduct. Even the ardent love of liberty will, after a time, give way to its dictates. The violent destruction of life and property incident to war, the continual effort and alarm attendant on a state of continual danger, will compel nations the most attached to liberty to resort for repose and security to institutions which have a tendency to destroy their civil and political rights. To be more safe, they at length become willing to run the risk of being less free."

I will now turn to my colleague, Mr. Watt, the distinguished Ranking Member of my Subcommittee and ask him if he has any opening remarks.

[The prepared statement of Mr. Cannon follows in the Appendix]

Mr. WATT. Thank you, Mr. Chairman. I thank the Chairman of this Committee and the Chairman of the Constitution Subcommittee for deciding to have a hearing on the issues involved today and to do it jointly so that we do not end up duplicating efforts and pulling in different directions possibly.

I would like to start really by expressing thanks to the witnesses for being here today. And by expressing a special thanks to Lee Hamilton and Slade Gordon, the members of the Commission, for the outstanding job that they did under some very, very, very difficult circumstances; and getting through the process without any appearance of partisanship, and being single-focused on the issue at hand, which was protecting American citizens and others from terrorism.

Who knows where the recommendations of the Commission will go? And it is hard to even contemplate where they may go legislatively or administratively. But the thing that I think is most important is that before they go anywhere, we understand exactly what the recommendations are and have a better understanding of all of the implications of the recommendations.

I sense that several Committees have headed off in the direction of dealing only with the security side of the balance that must be struck. And I think it is our obligation in this Committee not only to look at the security side, but to be ever cognizant of the privacy implications and the personal liberty implications of what is being done. And the only way we can do that is to really have hearings about what is being proposed and what we should be implementing.

I am extremely encouraged that the Commission recognize this delicate balance itself in its recommendations, making three specific recommendations pertaining to the protection of civil liberties. First, the report calls for the President to "safeguard the privacy of individuals about whom information is shared among intelligence and investigation agencies."

Second, the report requires that in order to retain a particular governmental power, the executive first demonstrate that the "power actually materially enhances security," and that adequate oversight exist "to ensure protection of civil liberties." so it is very apparent that the Commission is already wrestling with what the appropriate balance should be between safeguarding our citizens by protecting them from terrorism and, on the other hand, safeguarding our citizens by protecting them against overstepping by governmental agencies who say that they have our interests at heart.

So that is a very delicate balance which I think this hearing can only enlighten the American public on and enlighten the Members of this Committee on as we move forward, and enlighten our colleagues in the broader House and Senate as we move forward.

Finally, the report recommends the creation of a board within the executive branch to oversee adherence to the guidelines, and it recommends the commitment the Government makes to defend civil liberties. So that board is again supposed to walk that delicate balance between adhering to the guidelines and recommending a commitment to defend civil liberties. And I think that is absolutely critical as we move forward.

So I am delighted that the Chairman has convened this hearing for the purpose of discussing, and I hope nobody takes this as any indication that we in this Committee are not as committed to the defense of our citizens from terrorism, rather that they take it as an equal commitment that we understand the historical imperative, the constitutional imperative of also safeguarding the security and individual rights and privacy of citizens as we authorize the Government to take the actions that are necessary to safeguard us against terrorism.

That is going to be a very, very delicate balance to walk. And if we are going to do it, this is the place to start, right here in the Committee on the Judiciary, in the Constitution Subcommittee, in the Commerce and Administrative Law Subcommittee where it is our responsibility to look at these issues and make some very difficult choices.

I thank the Chairman and the members of the Commission and our other witnesses for being here to enlighten us on where that delicate balance should be.

Thank you, Mr. Chairman.

Mr. CANNON. Thank you, Mr. Watt.

Mr. CANNON. Mr. Watt and I have, on occasion, disagreed very sharply, and by "sharply," meaning he has a very sharp mind and it is hard to disagree with him.

On the other hand, there are many issues where we do not disagree at all and this is one of those areas where we have difficult issues and we may differ on some points, but we will come up with, I hope, some thoughtful resolutions. So I want to thank the minority Ranking Member.

I would also like to thank Mr. Chabot for being here today and his Ranking Member, Mr. Nadler.

Mr. Chabot, would you like to make a statement?

Mr. CHABOT. Thank you, Mr. Chairman. I first of all want to thank you for holding this hearing, as well as Mr. Watt, Mr. Nadler, the Ranking Member on the Subcommittee that I have the good fortune to chair; and I want to thank all of my Committee Members who are in attendance today. And I want to offer a special welcome to all of the witnesses, but especially the Honorable Congressman Hamilton whose district in Indiana abutted mine in the southwest corner of Ohio, in the time that I have been in Congress, for a number of years.

Lee was also the Chairman of the Committee on International Relations and served for many years with distinction. When my party took over in 1994, he was the Ranking Member for the time that I served here, but nonetheless he served with great distinction. He was really a role model for many of us, especially in the area of international affairs. So I want to thank him for his leadership in that respect.

Also, Senator Gorton, who served the people of Washington for so many years so well. I want to thank all of the witnesses for being here today.

I want to thank especially Senator Gorton and Senator Hamilton for the last 20 months that they have served on the 9/11 Commission. Our Nation owes you a great debt of gratitude for your work, and I am confident that we will all benefit from your expertise here this morning and in the future as we implement all or most of the recommendations that you have made.

As we know far too well, September 11 changed our world. It changed the way in which we must deal with terrorism and the way in which we as a country must protect ourselves. Since that tragic day, Congress and the Administration have taken steps to help better protect our Nation at home and abroad. Through passage of the PATRIOT Act and the creation of the Department of Homeland Security, we have provided law enforcement with enhanced investigative tools and improved our ability to coordinate abilities designed to protect against the future threat of terrorism. And make no mistake, that threat continues to face our Nation.

Through the heroic actions of the brave men and women serving in our Armed Forces, we have also pursued the terrorists and those who assist them in places like Afghanistan and Iraq. Yet these actions are not enough to guarantee our Nation's security or freedom. This can only be accomplished through continued vigilance and willingness to challenge conventional wisdom. We must continue to improve our intelligence capability, strengthen our defenses and always be a step ahead of our enemies.

To help accomplish these critical goals, it is imperative that Congress provide a comprehensive and expeditious review of the 9/11 Commission recommendations and then move forward with initiatives that will further improve our ability to combat terrorism and defend our citizens.

As the Commission notes, we must also be mindful of the protections afforded by our Constitution and our need to guard those protections as we work to better protect our country. Ignoring important civil liberties will not only erode our freedoms, but will undermine efforts to increase our security. These challenges are not new, and our two Subcommittees have been extensively involved in these issues over the last couple of years.

In the PATRIOT Act, for example, we worked to include protective measures such as a sunset provision to strengthen congressional oversight. When authorizing the Department of Homeland Security, a privacy officer position was established to examine the implications of the agency's rules and regulations on privacy and to address any issues that may result.

I look forward, as I know the other Members do, to discussing the Commission's recommendations with our witnesses today in determining what Congress can do to better protect the privacy of our citizens. I particularly look forward to hearing from our panel their views on the Federal Agency Privacy Protection Act of 2004, which passed the House during the 107th Congress and was recently voted out of the full Judiciary Committee. It was back on, I believe, July 7.

I believe that this, which was formerly known as the Defense of Privacy Act, would require Federal agencies to publish privacy impact analyses when promulgating rules and regulations. I believe it would be an effective step forward in our efforts to protect our country and our privacy rights.

As we move forward, it is important to remember that having effective antiterrorism measures does not necessarily compromise the protections afforded by our Constitution, as one is not the enemy of the other. The enemy is terrorism.

I yield back my time and thank the Chairman once again for holding this hearing.

Mr. CANNON. Thank you, Mr. Chairman. I thank you for that opening statement.

[The prepared statement of Mr. Chabot follows in the Appendix]

Mr. CANNON. Mr. Nadler, would you like to make an opening statement?

Mr. NADLER. Thank you, Mr. Chairman. Mr. Chairman, given the importance of this matter and the fact that nearly 3 years have elapsed since the attacks of September 11, I am pleased that we have returned to consider the recommendations of the 9/11 Commission now without waiting, as some have suggested, until next year.

I want to welcome our former colleagues Representative Hamilton and Senator Gorton and to thank them for the important work they and their colleagues have done.

I am also pleased that we have Secretary Marsh here today. The issues that gave rise to the Secretary's Technology and Privacy Advisory Committee are also implicated in the Committee's recommendation, so it is important that we have the benefit of our work.

Finally, I want to welcome back Ms. O'Connor Kelly. The 9/11 Commission has recommended in somewhat general terms that we set up a civil liberties oversight board. The TAPAC commission has similarly recommended that the Secretary of Defense create a policy level privacy officer. Congress will have to work out the details.

I hope that your experience as the privacy officer of the Department of Homeland Security can shed some light on how we might ensure the independence and effectiveness of the offices created pursuant to these recommendations.

The need to improve capabilities and coordination within the intelligence and law enforcement communities was all too well demonstrated on September 11. Thousands of innocent citizens who did nothing more than board an aircraft or go to work were barbarically slaughtered. We ignored our Nation's peril, the lesson we can draw from the intelligence failures leading up to those crimes and from other recent intelligence fiascoes.

At the same time, increased Government powers carry with them increased threats to the rights of all citizens. We expect our Government to keep it safe, but we are also a nation with a healthy mistrust of unfettered governmental power.

Our whole system of Government combines limited powers with checks and balances that must maintained. Rights sacrificed at a time of emergency are often lost forever. Actions taken in the heat of the moment are often a source of shame and regret to later generations. So our job is to strike an appropriate and workable balance.

That is not easy. As the members of the Commission have noted in their report, "While protecting our homeland, Americans should be mindful of threats to vital personal and civil liberties. This balancing is no easy task, but we must constantly strive to keep it right. This shift of power and authority to the Government calls for an enhanced systems of checks and balances to protect the precious liberties that are vital to our way of life."

A little further on the Commission notes, it talks in general terms about the provision of the PATRIOT Act and some of the beneficial provisions of the PATRIOT Act, and then it says, "Because of concerns regarding the shifting balance of power to the Government, we think that a full and informed debate on the PATRIOT Act would be healthy." The Commission then makes three general recommendations for specific measures to balance civil liberties and national security.

Mr. Justice Marshall in a noted decision of the Supreme Court 200 years ago in *Marbury* v. *Madison*, a decision that has been somewhat criticized by one Member of this Committee, noted, and I am paraphrasing here because I do not have the exact quote before me, "It is emphatically the province of the judiciary to say what the law is."

And that is true. It is emphatically the province of the Judiciary Committee to begin the process of having Congress strike the proper balance between national security, homeland security, and protection of our civil liberties. That is our job.

I appreciate the beginning guidance that the Commission has given us and recommended that we strike that balance, but we have to determine how to strike that balance. And I am glad and I appreciate the Chairman calling this hearing as a beginning of that process so we can carefully consider all of the things we have to consider to strike that balance, and with all deliberate speed, enact legislation to do that.

So I am glad we are having this hearing and I thank you.

Thank you, Mr. Chairman.

Mr. CANNON. I thank the gentleman.

[The prepared statement of Mr. Nadler follows in the Appendix]

Mr. CANNON. I would like to just point out to my co-Chair of this hearing, Mr. Chabot, Ranking Member Watt, and Ranking Member Nadler, we have worked together on issues not unlike this for some period of time, including the PATRIOT Act and other issues. And there is a genuine, I believe, feeling for doing the right thing here, and I hope that that will result in legislation in an area that is very, very difficult and improve that legislation.

Without objection, the gentlemen's entire statements will be placed in the record. Also, without objection, all Members may place their statements in the record at this point. Any objection?

Hearing none, so ordered.

Without objection, the Chair will be authorized to declare recesses of the hearing at any point. Hearing none, so ordered.

I ask unanimous consent that Members have 5 legislative days to submit written statements for inclusion in today's hearing record. Without objection, so ordered.

Mr. CANNON. Now I am pleased to introduce our witnesses for today's hearing. Our first witness is Lee Hamilton, who is Vice Chair of the 9/11 Commission. Former Congressman Hamilton currently is President and Director of the Woodrow Wilson International Center For Scholars. Before undertaking these responsibilities at the Center in 1999, Congressman Hamilton served for 34 years in the House, representing Indiana's Ninth District. During his tenure, he served as Chairman and Ranking Member of the forerunner of the House Committee on International Relations and served on the Permanent Select Committee on Intelligence and the Select Committee To Investigate Covert Arms Transactions with Iran.

After his tenure in Congress, he served on the Commission on National Security in the 21st Century, also known as the Hart-Rudman Commission, and was co-Chair with former Senator Howard Baker of the Baker-Hamilton Commission to investigate certain security issues at Los Alamos. He is currently a member of the President's Homeland Security Advisory Council.

Mr. Hamilton is a graduate of DePauw University and Indiana University Law School, as well as the recipient of numerous honorary degrees and national awards for public service. And I hope I have said privately to Mr. Hamilton what I would like to say now and that is that when I came to Congress I looked around at the various Members of Congress to decide who I wanted to model, he was very clearly one of the people who I think did a remarkably good job in a complex institution; and he has been an explicit model in my life in my office.

I welcome you back, Mr. Hamilton.

Our second witness is former Senator Slade Gorton who also appears on behalf of the 9/11 Commission. Senator Gorton is currently of counsel at Preston, Gates & Ellis. Prior to joining the firm, he represented Washington State in the United States Senate for 18 years, from 1982 to 2000. While in the Senate, Mr. Gorton served on the Appropriations, Budget, Commerce, Science and Transportation, and Energy and Natural Resources Committees. He also chaired the Interior Appropriations Subcommittee, and was a member of the Republican Leadership as Counsel to the Majority Leader.

Senator Gorton began his political career in 1958 as a Washington State representative and then went on to serve as the State house majority leader. In 1968, he was elected Attorney General for the State of Washington where he argued 14 cases before the United States Supreme Court. Mr. Gorton also served on the President's Consumer Advisory Council, as well as on many other Federal and State commissions. Most recently, Senator Gorton served on the National Commission on Federal Election Reform.

Senator Gorton received his undergraduate degree from Dartmouth College and his law degree from Columbia University.

We welcome you back and appreciate your service in the Senate where we had some very pleasant interactions over a period of time.

Our third witness is John Marsh, who appears today on behalf of TAPAC. Secretary Marsh, like his fellow witnesses, has served our Nation in a number of distinguished ways, I might just say a very different and a remarkable history of service, most prominently as Secretary of the Army and as the representative of Virginia's Seventh Congressional District. After an exemplary period of service with the U.S. Army, Secretary Marsh received his law degree in 1951 from Washington and Lee University and began his practice of law in Strasburg, VA. Thereafter, he was elected to four terms of Congress from the Seventh District of Virginia and served on the House Appropriations Committee.

After choosing not to seek a fifth term, Secretary Marsh resumed the practice of law. In 1973, however, he returned to Federal service as Assistant Secretary of Defense for Legislative Affairs. The following year, he became the Assistant for National Security Affairs to Vice President Ford, and in August 1974 became Counselor, with Cabinet rank, to President Ford. He chaired the Presidential Committee for the Reorganization of the U.S. Intelligence Community from 1975 to 1976.

Later sworn in as Secretary of the Army in 1981, Secretary Marsh served until 1989 achieving a tenure that was the longest of any Secretary of the Army or Secretary of War in American history. During 1988, he served concurrently as Assistant Secretary of Defense for Special Operations and Low Intensity Conflict.

Secretary Marsh has been awarded numerous honors and decorations. He is currently a Distinguished Professor of Law at George Mason University concentrating on cyberterrorism and national security law. He is also a member of the Special Congressional Panel on Terrorism to assess Federal, State and local response to weapons of mass destruction, known as the Gilmore Commission.

Our final witness is Nuala O'Connor Kelly, the Chief Privacy Officer at the Department of Homeland Security. We welcome you back.

As many of you know, Ms. O'Connor Kelly testified earlier this year as part of my Subcommittee's continuing oversight of her office. Ms. O'Connor Kelly is especially commended for participating in today's hearing as she is currently on maternity leave and having difficulty getting enough sleep. So we will send someone out for a coffee or a Coke if you need that at some point.

As I previously noted in my remarks, my Subcommittee with the support of our Chairman, Mr. Sensenbrenner, played a major role in establishing Ms. O'Connor Kelly's office at the Department of Homeland Security. The legislation creating her office not only mandated the appointment of a privacy officer, but specified the officer's responsibilities.

One of the principal responsibilities of the DHS privacy officer, as set out by statute, is the duty to assure that the use of technologies sustain and do not erode privacy protections relating to the use, collection and disclosure of personal information. In addition, the privacy officer must assure that personal information is handled in full compliance with the Privacy Act and assess privacy impacts with the Department's proposed rules.

Pursuant to this legislation, DHS Secretary Tom Ridge last year appointed Ms. O'Connor Kelly to serve as the Department's Chief Privacy Officer. Since her appointment, Ms. O'Connor Kelly has played a key role in various terrorist detection initiatives undertaken by DHS. Prior to her current appointment, she served as the Chief Privacy Officer at the Commerce Department.

Before entering public service, Ms. O'Connor Kelly was the Vice President for Data Protection and the Chief Privacy Officer for DoubleClick, an online media services company that made great headlines just prior to her taking that position.

In that capacity, Ms. O'Connor Kelly established the company's first data protection department responsible for instituting privacy protection policies and procedures for DoubleClick, its clients and partners.

Ms. O'Connor Kelly received her undergraduate degree from Princeton University, a Master's degree in Education from Harvard University and a law degree from Georgetown University Law Center.

I extend my warm regards and appreciate your willingness to participate in today's hearing. In light of the fact that your written statements will be included in the hearing record, I request that you limit your oral remarks to 5 minutes. Accordingly, please feel free to summarize or highlight the salient points of your testimony.

You will note that we have a lighting system. I think you are all familiar with it. It starts at green; when 4 minutes have passed, it turns yellow, and then it turns red at 1 minute. We do not want to cut off your thinking. In fact, I would like to say this is undoubtedly the most prestigious panel I will ever—we have had two justices from the Supreme Court recently testifying on the Administrative Conference of the United States, Justices Scalia and Breyer.

But there are only two of them and their history is fairly narrow compared with the experience we have with you.

So if you would just recognize the 5-minute light, we would appreciate it if you would draw to a close. We will have people that will have the opportunity to ask questions and expand on issues.

Everyone was here at the beginning of the hearing, so we will go by seniority. With Mr. Watts' help, I will try to tap the gavel at 5 minutes so all Members have an opportunity to ask questions. If there is an interest, we may go to a second round of questions.

Pursuant to the directive of the Chairman of the Committee on the Judiciary, I am going to ask the panel to stand and raise your right hand and take an oath.

[Witnesses sworn.]

Mr. CANNON. Congressman Hamilton, would you proceed with your testimony?

**TESTIMONY OF THE HONORABLE LEE H. HAMILTON, VICE CHAIR, NATIONAL COMMISSION ON TERRORIST ATTACKS UPON THE UNITED STATES**

Mr. HAMILTON. Thank you very much Chairman Cannon, Ranking Member Watt, Chairman Chabot, Ranking Member Nadler and the other distinguished Members of the two Subcommittees. We are very honored to appear before you today.

I want to say that the chairman of the 9/11 Commission, Tom Kean, was not able to be here today. He led the Commission with extraordinary skill and deserves much of the credit for the Commission's success.

I am very pleased to be here with Senator Gorton. He made extraordinary contributions as a Commission member. We turned to him again and again for advice, and it is a pleasure to be with him.

We especially appreciate the fact that all the Members are here during August. I know that it is unprecedented, and we are very grateful to you for your interest in our work.

I want to say that the statements made by the Chairman and Ranking Members of the two Subcommittees were extraordinarily good statements. I thank you for those. I also thank you for the personal sentiments that you expressed.

Your Subcommittees, as well as your parent Committee, have a very long record of concern and leadership in these issues, so it is a very special pleasure for us to be with you. We simply point out that our Commission's recommendations were unanimous. I think you know that.

I think from the very beginning of the Commission's work, about 18 or more months ago, all of us have been very conscious of the need to make sure that in our zeal to fight terrorism, we do not compromise the very rights and liberties that make our system of Government and society worth defending.

Concern about the civil liberties of American citizens was one of the number of reasons why the Commission rejected the idea of moving the domestic intelligence and counterterrorism responsibilities of the FBI out of that agency and placing them in an MI-5 type agency. We feared that such a new agency, not steeped in respect for law and the Constitution that pervades the FBI and the Justice Department, and reporting to the National Intelligence Director, the Director of Central Intelligence rather than the Attorney General, would be more likely to trample on individual rights.

The Commission made three major recommendations with respect to civil rights. The first dealt with the critical and complicated privacy issues that are at the heart of our new information society and at the heart of the necessary efforts to increase the amount of information gathered by our intelligence agencies and shared by them among themselves and with State and local law enforcement officials.

We recommend improvements and enhancements in those information gathering abilities and in information sharing. But we also recognize that with the enhanced flow of information comes a need to establish guidelines and oversight to make sure that the privacy of our citizens and residents is respected and preserved.

We did not conduct extensive investigation of our own on data mining and other privacy issues raised by information gathering and sharing. We relied very much on the Markle Task Force. I'm sure that work is familiar to you. We believe, along with the Markle Task Force, that we have the ability to gather and share information and protect privacy at the same time. This requires, however, leadership and coordination in the executive branch.

No one agency can deal with this problem alone. We recommend that the President lead a Government-wide effort through OMB and the National Intelligence Director to set common standards for information use throughout the Intelligence Community. These standards would govern the acquisition, accessing, sharing and using of private data so as to protect individual rights.

The same technology that facilitates the gathering and sharing of information can also protect us from the misuse of that information. And for the balance of the statement, I turn to Senator Gorton.

**TESTIMONY OF THE HONORABLE SLADE GORTON, COMMISSION MEMBER, NATIONAL COMMISSION ON TERRORIST ATTACKS UPON THE UNITED STATES**

Mr. GORTON. Our second major recommendation in this area relates to the USA PATRIOT Act, many of the provisions of which expire at the end of next year and will be the subject of hearings by the House and Senate Judiciary Committees. The only specific provisions of that act on which we expressed a view are those relating to information sharing.

The elimination of the wall that had severely constrained the flow of information acquired through surveillance under the Foreign Intelligence Surveillance Act from the intelligence side of the FBI and to the criminal side of the Agency and to Federal prosecutors, and the broadening of the ability of the Justice Department to share grand jury information with other intelligence and law enforcement agencies.

We endorse the extension of those provisions which, witnesses were virtually unanimous in telling us, were extremely helpful to law enforcement and intelligence investigations with little, if any, adverse impact on the rights of potential defendants. But we did propose a general test to be applied to consideration of the renewal of the other provisions of the USA PATRIOT Act, and we believe that that principle should also be applied to other legislative and regulatory proposals designed to strengthen our security, but that may impinge on individual rights.

The test is a simple but important one. The burden of proof should be on the proponents of the measure to establish that the power or authority being sought would, in fact, materially enhance national security, and that there will be adequate supervision of the exercise of that power or authority to ensure protection of civil liberties. If the power is granted, there must be adequate guidelines and oversight properly to confine its use.

We think that the same spirit that informed our recommendation as to the burden of proof that should be applied to measures of this kind is also reflected in H.R. 338, recently reported out of this Subcommittee and the full Judiciary Committee. H.R. 338 requires Federal agencies that are proposing rules that will require the collection of personal information from individuals to conduct privacy impact assessments as part of their rule-making process to ensure that privacy interests of individuals receive attention and protection.

The Commission, of course, takes no position on that bill. But we can observe that it proceeds from the same concerns that animate our recommendations.

Our third recommendation flows from the first two. Individual rights and liberties must be adequately protected in the administration of the significant powers that Congress has granted to executive branch agencies to protect national security. There should be a central office or board that has the responsibility to oversee adherence guidelines that are built into these programs to safeguard these rights and liberties.

We make no recommendation as to how this office or board should be composed or where in the executive branch it should be located. Some commissioners believe that it should be a permanent office located in the Justice Department and reporting to the Attorney General, but with oversight of the programs of the Department of Homeland Security and other agencies, as well as those of the Justice Department. Others envisage a Cabinet-level interagency board or committee reporting to the President. But we are all agreed that some entity of this kind should be created.

And departing for just a moment from my written statement, both the Chairman and Mr. Watt referred to the importance of this vehicle. Yesterday, Mr. Lee Hamilton and I testified before the Senate Judiciary Committee. Thereafter, I made a contact I'd made previously with Senators McCain and Lieberman who are working on a bill to provide exactly this board.

I went and spoke at length with the staff director of the Senate Commerce Committee, formerly a member of my staff, on such a draft. And it may well be that you would like to contact them, see the direction in which they are going and work together. It looked to me like a very constructive first draft.

We close with an observation from our report. We must find ways of reconciling security with liberty since the success of one protects the other. The choice between security and liberty is a false choice as nothing is more likely to endanger America's liberties than the success of a terrorist attack at home. Our history has shown us that insecurity threatens liberty. Yet, if our liberties are concerned, we lose the values that we are struggling to defend.

We will be pleased to respond to your questions.

Mr. CANNON. Thank you, Mr. Hamilton and Mr. Gorton.

[The prepared statement of Messrs. Hamilton and Gorton follows:]

PREPARED STATEMENT OF LEE HAMILTON AND SLADE GORTON

Chairman Cannon, Ranking Member Watt, and other distinguished members of the Subcommittee: We are honored by the opportunity to appear before you today. We appreciate the opportunity to discuss with you the findings and recommendations of the Commission with respect to privacy and civil liberties. These Subcommittees, as well as your parent Committee, have a long record of concern with these issues, so it is a special pleasure to discuss with you the important question of how the measures we must take to protect our nation against the threat of terrorist attacks can be reconciled with the individual rights and liberties we hold so dear.

We want to emphasize that the Commission's views on these issues—as well as all others dealt with in our Report—were unanimous. We are five Republicans and five Democrats, but we are united in our commitment to make our country safer and more secure in the face of the novel threat posed by transnational terrorism. And we can report to you that from the very beginning of the Commission's work some eighteen months ago, all of us have been conscious of the need to make sure that in our zeal to fight the scourge of terrorism we do not compromise the very rights and liberties that make our system of government and our society worth defending.

Concern about the civil liberties of American citizens was one of a number of reasons why the Commission rejected the idea of moving the domestic intelligence and counterterrorism responsibilities of the FBI out of that agency and placing them in a new MI-5-type agency. We feared that such a new agency, not steeped in the respect for the law and the Constitution that pervades the FBI and the Justice Department, and reporting to the National Intelligence Director or the Director of Central Intelligence rather than to the Attorney General, would be more likely to trample on individual rights.

The Commission made three major recommendations with respect to civil liberties. The first dealt with the critical and complicated privacy issues that are at the heart of our new "information society" and at the heart of the necessary efforts to increase the amount of information gathered by our intelligence agencies and shared by them among themselves and with state and local law enforcement officials. The Commission recommends improvements and enhancements in those information-gathering abilities and in information sharing. But we also recognize that with the enhanced flow of information comes a need to establish guidelines and oversight to make sure that the privacy of our citizens and residents is respected and preserved.

We did not conduct extensive investigation of our own on data-mining and other privacy issues raised by information gathering and sharing. Instead, we relied on the excellent work done by the Markle Foundation Task Force, reflected in two reports, in 2002 and 2003. The insights of the Markle Task Force have been reinforced by the more recent investigation and report by the Technology and Privacy Advisory Committee established by Secretary Rumsfeld to advise him on the privacy implications of the Department's Terrorism Information Awareness Program—a report that this Subcommittee is also focusing on today.

We believe, along with the Markle Task Force, that we have the ability to gather and share information and protect privacy at the same time. But this requires leadership and co-ordination in the executive branch. No one agency can deal with this problem alone. Instead, we recommend that the President lead a government-wide effort, through OMB and the National Intelligence Director, to set common standards for information use throughout the intelligence community. These standards would govern the acquisition, accessing, sharing and using of private data so as to protect individual rights. The same technology that facilitates the gathering and sharing of information can also protect us from the misuse of that information.

Our second major recommendation in this area relates to the USA PATRIOT Act, many of the provisions of which expire at the end of next year and will be the subject of hearings by the House and Senate Judiciary Committees. The only specific provisions of that Act on which we expressed a view are those relating to information-sharing: the elimination of the "wall" that had severely constrained the flow of information acquired through surveillance under the Foreign Intelligence Surveillance Act from the intelligence side of the FBI to the criminal side of the agency and to federal prosecutors, and the broadening of the ability of the Justice Department to share grand jury information with other intelligence and law enforcement agencies. We endorsed the extension of those provisions, which witnesses were virtually unanimous in telling us were extremely helpful to law enforcement and intelligence investigations with little if any adverse impact on the rights of potential defendants.

But we did propose a general test to be applied to consideration of the renewal of other provisions of the USA PATRIOT Act, and we believe that that principle should also be applied to other legislative and regulatory proposals that are designed to strengthen our security but that may impinge on individual rights. The test is a simple but important one: The burden of proof should be on the proponents of the measure to establish that the power or authority being sought would in fact materially enhance national security, and that there will be adequate supervision of the exercise of that power or authority top ensure protection of civil liberties. If the power is granted, there must be adequate guidelines and oversight to properly confine its use.

We think the same spirit that informed our recommendation as to the burden of proof that should be applied to measures of this kind is also reflected in H.R. 338, recently reported out of this Subcommittee and the full Judiciary Committee. H.R. 338 requires federal agencies that are proposing rules that will require the collection of personal information from individuals to conduct privacy impact assessments as part of their rulemaking process to ensure that privacy interests of individuals receive attention and protection. The Commission, of course, takes no position on that bill. But we can observe that it proceeds from the same concerns that animate our recommendations.

Our third major recommendation flows from the first two. Individual rights and liberties must be adequately protected in the administration of the significant powers that Congress has granted to executive branch agencies to protect national security. There should be a central office or board that has the responsibility to oversee adherence to guidelines that are built into these programs to safeguard those rights and liberties. We make no recommendation as to how this office or board should be composed or where in the executive branch it should be located. Some Commissioners believe that it should be a permanent office located in the Justice Department and reporting to the Attorney General, but with oversight of programs in the Department of Homeland Security and other agencies as well as in the Justice Department. Others envision a Cabinet-level interagency board or committee, reporting to the President. But we are all agreed that some entity of this kind should be created.

We close with an observation from our Report:

> We must find ways of reconciling security with liberty, since the success of one protects the other. The choice between security and liberty is a false choice, as nothing is more likely to endanger America's liberties than the success of a terrorist attack at home. Our history has shown us that insecurity threatens liberty. Yet, if our liberties are curtailed, we lose the values that we are struggling to defend.

We would be pleased to respond to your questions.

Mr. CANNON. Mr. Marsh.

## TESTIMONY OF THE HONORABLE JOHN O. MARSH, JR., MEMBER, U.S. DEPARTMENT OF DEFENSE TECHNOLOGY AND PRIVACY ADVISORY COMMITTEE

Mr. MARSH. Thank you, Mr. Chairman, Members of the Committee and leaders of the Committee. I thank you for calling this hearing. I would point out to you that I am here representing an advisory committee appointed by Secretary of Defense to the Department of Defense composed of members who gave their time to make this study. Therefore, I am not speaking for the Department of Defense of what action may or may not occur in reference to our recommendations, but I am very sanguine about that.

I would also like to point out, as resource people for the committee, which I hope you will avail yourself of, the staff director of the Defense TAPAC Committee, Ms. Lisa Davis; an extraordinary writer, Fred Cate, who helped prepare all this testimony; a technologist and attorney, Lee Zeichner, who is here, and also the critical infrastructure protection capabilities of George Mason University where I teach and that assisted in this.

Mr. Minow could not be here, but I can tell you he performed a yeoman's task of guiding this committee, and his enormous prestige and ability I think is reflected in this work.

A little history, if I might. This committee occurred because of what was discerned to be abuses, or concerns about abuses, largely outside of the Department of Defense on a common technique that is growing and needs to be addressed called "data mining." Data mining is the result of massive volumes of information, either people in or out of Government or organizations, and the use of that data mining can be very, very helpful in the intelligence process.

There is a dichotomy here because although the Defense Department got in trouble with the pursuit of this, nevertheless, the statute to the homeland security authorized and encouraged them to engage in data processing. The data processing that was occurring in the Pentagon was called TIA. Its original name was terrorism information awareness or total information awareness or terrorist information awareness, whichever one you want, but it raised very serious questions in the media and in the Congress of the United States.

When that happened, Mr. Rumsfeld named this committee, and he gave them six questions that he wished to be answered as to the validity of that type of technology and whether it could be effective, and how do we protect individual liberty and privacy.

Incidentally, I prefer the term "liberty." It is a far stronger word than "privacy." Privacy occurs because of liberty. Privacy is a subset of liberty.

Now, these four questions were the questions to which we devoted our time and attention. And our first overtures were to TIA, which was being done under DARPA, the Defense Advanced Research Project Agency, that has done extraordinary work and is indeed the agency that developed the Internet. It became apparent to the committee that to address this one program, TIA, would be putting a finger in a dike where many, many fingers were going to be necessary.

This is a widespread practice in the Federal Government and perhaps at State levels. A GAO survey indicated, as we were finishing up our work, that there were 88 departments and agencies engaged in data mining, or were planning to, that there were an additional 34 about to, and in all, there were 122 data mining programs ongoing in our national Government, not just in the Department of Defense. It became very apparent to us, as we began to examine people, that data mining was going on in other departments of Government. And there weren't that many controls in my view and, I think, in the committee view as to how that should be handled.

So what we sought to do—this report is seeking to provide some guidelines as to how to utilize data mining, which we think is essential only if it is used in a proper way, and we believe that it can be. It can use the FICE Accord. It can use technologies of minimization where in order to achieve certain information you do not have to collect as much as you perceive that you have to collect.

And also, there is the issue of anonymization. There are technologies today in seeking records, you can anonymize the records so that the people examining the records or capturing the information do not know—do not know at the time what that information is or they do not associate it with an individual. At a later date, under certain guidelines, you can unlock that and find that out.

But one of the things, and it seems to me to be a rule, where U.S. persons are involved and you have a particularized area of interest in that U.S. person and you go into data mining, you use and resort to the FICE Accord. We place stress or emphasis on the role of the FICE Accord.

Now, out of this would come—and I submit to the Committee that I will not go through it all; your staff has seen it—there came 12 recommendations. Seven of those recommendations relate to the Department of Defense, because it was the Department of Defense that had asked for these inputs. Five of those relate to the Federal Government at large.

I was very impressed with the legislation that's proposed, H.R. 338, that came out of this Committee, because as you read our report and read the proposed statute, you begin to see that there's a synchronization or there's a common theme through there. It may not be the answer yet, but it seems to me steps toward an answer.

So we talk about here how you can establish a process for data mining inside the Department of Defense. And the idea was, you create a mechanism in the Department of Defense that has audit trails, that has overview, that has training, that has authorization for certain techniques, and then you extrapolate that and replicate those systems of protection into the general Federal Government. And this evolved because we got in, we saw we had a far, far greater problem.

It is not simply the Department of Defense, but there are other departments and agencies of the Government, and indeed data mining is done by the States. The program called Matrix, which is a law enforcement program in the State of Florida, uses data mining; and Matrix, I think you will find, has significant Federal funding from certain other Federal agencies, not the Department of Defense.

But we also place an emphasis on congressional oversight of what's to be done. There needs to be a protocol or culture of privacy that we need to encourage and develop. So we commend those to you.

I thank you for what you're doing. The stakes are very, very high. As I commented to my assistant professor, Ms. Angie Chen of George Mason University, who is here today, "the law is going to have to address this."

In September of 1787, as Washington was submitting the draft Constitution to the convention, of the articles—to the Congress—of the Confederation, it had a resolution in it. I commend to you that resolution because it read, and it was Washington's dilemma, a resolution probably written by Madison.

Washington fully concurred. The biggest problem, Washington said, was drafting a document that was able to reconcile the issue of liberty on one side and security on the other.

That's the problem that we have today. And we see our Nation's capital, the people's House is a citadel, with the Jersey walls and hydraulic gates and the limitation. Visitation here used to be about 22,500. It is down now I understand to about 2,000. These are evidences of the oppression and intimidation that we are having to suffer because of the problems with terrorism. But we will address that and we will—and we will be stronger for it.

I would say to you, I was teaching these issues before 9/11. We are feeling that we are being overwhelmed by rapid advances in technology, particularly in the information communication and information technology which gives the terrorists enormous weapons.

Prior to 9/11, we would not sort out how we were going to handle that, and the law was falling behind that technology. And the Congress at the time was having trouble coming to grips with it in a jurisdictional sense because of its pervasive effort. Hopefully, through these types of efforts, we will, one, be able to establish jurisdiction, and, secondly, be able to achieve a very favorable and satisfactory result.

I thank you, Mr. Chairman.

Mr. CANNON. Thank you, Mr. Marsh.

[The prepared statement of Mr. Marsh follows:]

PREPARED STATEMENT OF JOHN O. MARSH, JR.[1]

Chairmen Chabot and Cannon, Distinguished Members:

I appreciate the opportunity to testify today about the work and final recommendations of the Technology and Privacy Advisory Committee appointed by Secretary of Defense Rumsfeld and chaired by the Honorable Newton N. Minow, one of the nation' most experienced and distinguished public servants. The Committee was created to examine the issues that are the subject of today's hearing—the impact of the government's use of personal information on privacy and civil liberties. Although our charge focused on the Department of Defense, we rapidly discovered that the issues, as well as the data mining activities that raise them, occur throughout the government and require attention.

I applaud your leadership and that of your colleagues on the Committee in holding today's hearing. As a former Member of Congress and Secretary of the Army, I know that few issues could be more important than the security of the Republic or the civil liberties of its citizens. Ensuring that both are rigorously protected is a critical obligation of all branches of Government—but especially of the Congress—and I congratulate you for embracing that responsibility in this hearing today.

THE TENSION BETWEEN PRIVACY AND NATIONAL SECURITY

The final report of the 9/11 Commission report does a masterful job of describing the horrendous terrorist attacks that took place on the morning of September 11, 2001, and of analyzing the factors that contributed to our nation's vulnerability to those attacks. The report goes on to make a number of thoughtful recommendations, including the urgent need that we use all of the information at our collective disposal to protect against further attacks, but that we do so only in ways that are consistent with protecting personal privacy.

The 9/11 Commission report does not suggest *how* we might exploit that information without invading privacy. The report identifies the goal, without providing any guidance as to the means. The Technology and Privacy Committee had spent the prior year addressing many of these issues about how we use information to protect national security without infringing on privacy.

[1] I gratefully acknowledge the assistance in the preparation of this statement of Fred H. Cate, a Distinguished Professor and director of the Indiana University Center for Applied Cybersecurity Research, who served as Reporter for the Technology and Privacy Advisory Committee.

BACKGROUND OF TAPAC

The history of TAPAC is fully laid out in our final report, the executive summary from which I attach to my prepared testimony, so I will only briefly recite it here. In early 2002, the Defense Advanced Research Projects Agency ("DARPA") announced that it was developing advanced information technologies which could access personally identifiable information in the fight against terrorism. The project—called "Terrorism Information Awareness" ("TIA")[2] soon prompted serious public and congressional criticism centered on the possible use by government of personal information on U.S. citizens and permanent resident aliens.

To address these and other concerns, in February 2003 Secretary Rumsfeld appointed the Technology and Privacy Advisory Committee, the members of which were private citizens, independent from the government and "selected on the basis of their preeminence in the fields of constitutional law and public policy relating to communication and information management." *Establishment of the Technology and Privacy Advisory Committee,* 68 Fed. Reg. 11,384 (2003) (DOD, notice). He charged TAPAC with answering four questions:

1. Should the goal of developing technologies that may help identify terrorists before they act be pursued?
2. What safeguards should be developed to ensure that the application of this or any like technology developed within DOD is carried out in accordance with U.S. law and American values related to privacy?
3. Which public policy goals are implicated by TIA and what steps should be taken to ensure that TIA does not frustrate those goals?
4. How should the government ensure that the application of these technologies to global databases respects international and foreign domestic law and policy? U.S. Department of Defense, *Technology and Privacy Advisory Committee Charter* (2003).

In June 2004, TAPAC released its final report, containing its conclusions and 7 and 5 12 recommendations addressing data mining within the Department of Defense and throughout the federal government. Before turning to those conclusions and recommendations, I want to stress two features of the Committee and its work.

First, the panel was strictly bi-partisan, both in its membership and in the way it pursued its work. It was chaired by the Honorable Newton N. Minow, Senior Counsel to the law firm of Sidley Austin Brown & Wood, who served as chairman of the Federal Communications Commission under President Kennedy, and later served as chairman of the Carnegie Corporation, Public Broadcasting Service, and The RAND Corporation, and vice chairman of the Commission on Presidential Debates. It would be hard to find a more impartial, skillful, or experienced public servant.

The other Committee members with whom I was privileged to serve were:

Floyd Abrams, a partner in the New York law firm of Cahill Gordon & Reindel, the William J. Brennan, Jr. Visiting Professor of First Amendment Law at the Columbia Graduate School of Journalism, and one of the nation's leading experts on the First Amendment.

Zoë Baird, President of the Markle Foundation, and previously was senior vice president and general counsel of Aetna, Inc., and an attorney in White House and in the Justice Department.

Griffin Bell, formerly Managing Partner of King & Spalding, a judge on the U.S. Court of Appeals for the Fifth Circuit, and Attorney General of the United States.

Gerhard Casper, President Emeritus of Stanford University and the Peter and Helen Bing Professor in Undergraduate Education at Stanford.

William T. Coleman, Jr., Senior Partner and the Senior Counselor in O'Melveny and Myers; he served as Secretary of Transportation during the Ford Administration.

Lloyd N. Cutler, founding partner of the law firm of Wilmer, Cutler & Pickering; he served as Counsel to Presidents Clinton and Carter.

The second feature is that Secretary Rumsfeld charged the Committee with considering not only laws applicable to privacy, but also "American values related to privacy." This important addition to the Committee's mandate obligated us to ask

[2] When first announced, the program was entitled "Total Information Awareness." The title was changed to "Terrorism Information Awareness" in May 2003.

not only what the law concerning government use of personal information was, but what it *should* be.

THE PREVALENCE OF GOVERNMENT DATA MINING AND THE LIMITS OF RELEVANT LAW

From the outset, the Committee was struck by two discoveries. The first was how widespread, not only in the Department of Defense, but throughout the federal government, data mining was. In fact, report by the General Accounting Office, released in May 2004 after the TAPAC finished its work, found 42 federal departments or agencies—including every cabinet-level agency that responded to the GAO's survey—engaged in (88), or were planning to engage in (34), 122 data mining efforts involving personal information. Thirty-six of those involve accessing data from the private sector; 46 involve sharing data among federal agencies. U.S. General Accounting Office, *Data Mining: Federal Efforts Cover a Wide Range of Uses* (GAO–04–548), May 2004, at 3, 27–64, tables 2–25.

The Committee's second discovery was how limited the federal law applicable to the government's use of personal information really was. The law that does exist is often too narrow to ensure either that the government can access the data it really needs to protect national security and fight crime effectively or that individual privacy is protected in the process. In particular, that law depends significantly on whether the individual(s) involved are U.S. citizens, where the search takes place, whether the information has ever been disclosed to third parties, and the government's motivation for the search. In the face of new terrorist threats posed within the territory of the United States and global information technologies this system has grown increasingly unworkable.

So what the Committee found was widespread data mining, and little clarity in the law.

TAPAC'S RECOMMENDATIONS

As a result, the Committee focused its deliberations, and ultimately its recommendations, on what the law should be to ensure that information is used to enhance national security without impinging on individual privacy or liberty. We unanimously agreed that the United States should use data mining to enhance national security; our recommendations then were focused on assuring that the privacy interests of U.S. persons are not compromised when it does so. Because those recommendations are included in the attached executive summary, I will not recite all of them here, but I would like to focus on six that are most relevant to today's hearing.

*1. Privacy Tools*

First, we thought it imperative that government data mining programs take advantage of the technological and other tools available to protect privacy. So, for example, we recommended requiring:

a. Data minimization—the least data consistent with the purpose of the data mining should be accessed, disseminated, and retained.
b. Data anonymization—whenever practicable data mining should be performed on databases from which information by which specific individuals can be commonly identified (e.g., name, address, telephone number, SSN, unique title, etc.) has been removed, encrypted, or otherwise obscured. Where it is not practicable to use anonymized data, or access to identifying information is required, the agency should comply with Recommendation 2.4 below.
c. Audit trail—data mining systems should be designed to create a permanent, tamper-resistant record of when data have been accessed and by whom.
d. Security and access—data mining systems should be secured against accidental or deliberate unauthorized access, use, alteration, or destruction, and access to such systems should be restricted to persons with a legitimate need and protected by appropriate access controls taking into account the sensitivity of the data.
e. Training—all persons engaged in developing or using data mining systems should be trained in their appropriate use and the laws and regulations applicable to their use. (Recommendation 2.2)

We also recommended special protection when data mining would involve the use of data from the private sector or other government agencies. (Recommendation 2.3)

*2. Privacy Culture*

Second, we thought it was critical that concern for privacy and other civil liberties be instilled at every level within agencies that engage in data mining. We therefore proposed that agency personnel receive appropriate training (Recommendation 2.2(e)), the creation of a policy-level privacy officer to help promote sensitivity to privacy throughout agencies (Recommendation 4), the appointment of external privacy advisors to help provide privacy-related input from outside of the agency (Recommendation 5), and that the agency head be charged specifically with creating "culture of sensitivity to, and knowledge about, privacy issues" throughout the agency (Recommendation 7).

*3. Internal Accountability*

Third, we believed that accountability was absolutely critical to protecting privacy, to ensuring that data mining was conducted efficiently and effectively, and to building public confidence in the government's data mining efforts. This objective undergirded many of our recommendations. We thought of accountability as occurring in two distinct settings: internal and external.

Internal accountability would be enhanced, we believed, first by ensuring that no agency engage in data mining involving personal information without making a conscious, thoughtful decision to do so, or without fully appreciating the potential privacy ramifications of its actions. So, for example, we recommended that data mining require written authorization by the agency head. (Recommendation 2.1) That written finding would demonstrate that a senior government official had thought through:

a. the purposes for which the system may be used;
b. the need for the data to accomplish that purpose;
c. the specific uses to which the data will be put;
d. that the data are appropriate for that use, taking into account the purpose(s) for which the data were collected, their age, and the conditions under which they have been stored and protected;
e. that other equally effective but less intrusive means of achieving the same purpose are either not practically available or are already being used;
f. the effect(s) on individuals identified through the data mining (e.g., they will be the subject of further investigation for which a warrant will be sought, they will be subject to additional scrutiny before being allowed to board an aircraft, etc.)
g. that the system has been demonstrated to his or her satisfaction to be effective and appropriate for that purpose;
h. that the system complies with the other requirements of this recommendation as enacted by law, executive order, or other means;
i. that the system yields a rate of false positives that is acceptable in view of the purpose of the search, the severity of the effect of being identified, and the likelihood of further investigation; and
j. that there is a system in place for dealing with false positives (e.g., reporting false positives to developers to improve the system, correcting incorrect information if possible, remedying the effects of false positives as quickly as practicable, etc.), including identifying the frequency and effects of false positives. (Recommendation 2.1)

That written finding would also serve to ensure that a policy-level official (in almost every case an official whose appointment was subject to Senate confirmation), was involved in making the determination to go forward.

We believed internal accountability would also be fostered through the creation of a senior policy-level privacy officer (Recommendation 5), by regular audits of all data mining programs (Recommendation 2.5), by seeking the advice of external privacy experts (Recommendation 5), and through renewed efforts by the agency head to ensure the "effective operation of meaningful oversight mechanisms" (Recommendation 6).

*4. External Accountability*

Fourth, while accountability within an agency is essential, it is no substitute for external accountability, and it was here that our strongest—and most controversial—recommendations were focused. I suspect it is the failure to provide for meaningful external accountability that has contributed to public unrest about programs such as TIA and CAPPS II. Our goal was to help diffuse some of that controversy in the future by providing for meaningful external oversight.

TAPAC recognized that programs to enhance national security and public safety will often involve classified information or require speedy action, and so traditional accountability measures (such as public notice and opportunity to comment, or judicial review) may not work. Nevertheless, we believed that significant tools are available and should be required when the government accesses personal information about its citizens or legal aliens.

a. Judicial Review

One critical external accountability measure we recommended is recourse to the courts before conducting data mining with personally identifiable information about U.S. persons. (Recommendation 2.4) We recommended the Foreign Intelligence Surveillance Act court, to help provide for speedy and confidential review, but the particular court is not nearly as important as the concept of judicial review. The public understandably derives confidence from knowing that an independent, judicial authority is reviewing government data mining efforts. This is especially true when, because of secrecy concerns, the public may not have access to information about those efforts.

We stressed that judicial review could be obtained for specific searches or for entire data mining programs (Recommendation 2.4(a)(v)), and we provided that, in exigent circumstances, the review could be obtained after-the-fact (Recommendation 2.4(c)). Our goal in crafting these provisions was not merely to ensure that the process of judicial review not interfere with national security, but also to highlight that even the exigencies of the war on terrorism do not justify abandoning the vital principle of judicial review.

b. Congressional Oversight

The other essential component of external accountability is oversight by the Congress. You are the people's elected representatives and it is your unique duty to ensure that the people's business is carried out effectively, efficiently, and without compromising the people's rights. TAPAC therefore recommended that each agency's privacy officer have a direct reporting line to Congress, as you provided with regard to the Department of Homeland Security's privacy officer—a position ably filled by Ms. Nuala O'Connor Kelly, who appeared before TAPAC. We went a step further, however, to recommend that the agency head appear as well, and that the privacy officer and agency head jointly brief you, at least annually, on

a. the agency's compliance with applicable privacy laws;
b. the number and nature of data mining systems within the agency, the purposes for which they are used, and whether they are likely to contain individually identifiable information about U.S. persons;
c. the number and general scope of agency findings authorizing data mining;
d. the number and general scope of agency findings and court orders authorizing searches of individually identifiable information about U.S. persons; and
e. other efforts to protect privacy in the agency's collection and use of U.S. person data. (Recommendation 11)

These are serious obligations; we meant them to be. Nothing less guarantees you the information and regular access to senior personnel necessary to provide the accountability that the public expects.

To carry out these obligations, we made an equally bold recommendation that you take the steps necessary to streamline committee jurisdiction:

> To facilitate this reporting process and consistent, knowledgeable oversight, each house of Congress should identify a single committee to receive all of the agencies' reports. Other committees may have jurisdiction over specific agencies and therefore also receive reports from those agencies, but we believe it is important for a single committee in each house to maintain broad oversight over the full range of federal government data mining activities. To the extent the jurisdiction of congressional committees overlaps, we believe it is essential for Congress to clarify and clearly articulate the relative responsibilities of each committee, to avoid undermining either privacy protection or national security efforts. (Recommendation 11)

As a former Member of Congress, I am well aware of the uphill battle that such an effort involves, but we believed it is essential for meaningful oversight of both privacy and security.

*5. Consistent Laws and Processes*

Fifth, TAPAC recommended that all of the actions outlined above be carried out across the government. This would include adopting a single framework of legal, technological, training, and oversight mechanisms necessary to guarantee the privacy of U.S. persons in the context of national security and law enforcement activities; the appointment of a privacy officer in every federal agency; and the creation of an inter-agency coordinating committee and the use of external advisors to help ensure the consistent application of privacy laws and principles. (Recommendations 8–10)

TAPAC recognized that privacy protections would not necessarily be the same in every setting, but we believed it essential that they be consistent, based on common principles, and subject to uniform oversight.

The recent report of the 9/11 Commission only highlights the importance of these recommendations. It makes little sense to coordinate this nation's intelligence and national security activities, without going one step further to coordinate the laws and processes that ensure those activities respect our privacy and civil liberties.

*6. Research*

Finally, TAPAC recognized the importance of research into technological and other tools for making data mining more precise and accurate and for protecting privacy, as well as into the development of policies and laws to facilitate both data mining and privacy. (Recommendations 7, 12) One unfortunate consequence of Congress blocking further development of TIA was to prohibit further research by DARPA into both data mining and privacy.

This is regrettable; our nation desperately needs to understand better the technological, behavioral, and policy tools for using information effectively and appropriately, whether to fight terrorism, apprehend criminals, or otherwise serve the public. There are many private initiatives to expand our understanding—my own program at the George Mason School of Law is one example—but if we are serious about using information to fight terrorism and serious about protecting privacy while doing so, it is going to require the investment of public funds.

## THE LINK BETWEEN PRIVACY AND NATIONAL SECURITY

I began by describing the tension between privacy and national security; I would now like to highlight what TAPAC saw as the essential link between the two. Many of our recommendations that may have been motivated by a desire to protect privacy, also contribute to enhancing security as well. Data minimization, for example, is a key privacy tool, but it also helps protect intelligence agencies from being overwhelmed by irrelevant data. Tools for data correction are another example: data mining with inaccurate data certainly threatens privacy and civil liberties, but it also threatens security as well. Any system of data analysis that is not concerned with data quality and accuracy is likely to compromise both privacy and security.

Privacy and national security are also inherently linked because American values will not accept the latter at the cost of the former. Recent protests over TIA, CAPPS II, and other programs have shown that the American public will not either. Inadequate, unclear, or uncertain privacy laws are slowing the development of new and promising data mining programs, they are undermining research into this important weapon in the war on terrorism, and they are hampering the very data sharing that the 9/11 Commission wisely recommended. Clearing up this mess is critical *both* to protecting our privacy *and* to protecting our security.

## THE ROLE OF THE JUDICIARY COMMITTEE

TAPAC took no position on which committee in Congress should take the lead on this vital effort, but I believe the Committee on the Judiciary is an ideal choice. The issues involve come within the jurisdiction of many committees—Armed Services, Intelligence, Commerce, Ways and Means, and others—but the foundational issue that cuts across all of these different settings is the constitutional and legal framework applicable to data mining. That is the fundamental question—the starting place for all other analysis. That is your turf. And I assume that is why you have called these important hearings today.

## CONCLUSION

Throughout Washington, throughout the nation, citizens are lining up to be searched before entering federal buildings or boarding aircraft. The mail is delayed so it can be scanned. Luggage is x-rayed and rummaged through. Roads are closed, entrances blocked with concrete barricades, access to public resources denied. Surveillance cameras and identity checks are replacing anonymity. The result is not just inconvenience or annoyance, it is a vast toll on our economy and productivity and a profound intrusion on our privacy and most basic civil liberties.

Think of the effect on government. The threat of terrorism has turned the People's House into an armed citadel. The Capitol, the very heart of democratic government, is under siege, and with it our privacy, liberty, and most cherished values.

Data mining—as both the 9/11 Commission and TAPAC noted—is a vital weapon in the war on terrorism. It poses grave risks to privacy, but there are numerous steps, many (but certainly not all) of which are outlined in the TAPAC report, that can reduce or eliminate those risks. Those steps may not only protect privacy, but also enhance security as well. More importantly, when pursued effectively and subject to appropriate safeguards, data mining may threaten privacy and civil liberties far less than the other tools on which we rely so heavily and so regrettably today.

Thank you.

**ATTACHMENT**

Enter
Safeguarding Privacy
in the
Fight Against Terrorism
REPORT OF THE TECHNOLOGY AND PRIVACY ADVISORY COMMITTEE
Executive Summary
March 2004

# SAFEGUARDING PRIVACY IN THE FIGHT AGAINST TERRORISM

**The Report of the Technology and Privacy Advisory Committee**

*Executive Summary*

MARCH 2004

DEPARTMENT OF DEFENSE
TECHNOLOGY AND PRIVACY ADVISORY COMMITTEE
3330 Defense Pentagon, Room 3E1045
Washington, DC 20301-3330



March 1, 2004

The Hon. Donald H. Rumsfeld
Secretary of Defense
Department of Defense
1000 Defense Pentagon 3E880
Washington, DC 20301-1000

Dear Secretary Rumsfeld:

In February 2003, you appointed the Technology and Privacy Advisory Committee to examine the Terrorism Information Awareness program and to develop safeguards "to ensure that the application of this or any like technology developed within DOD is carried out in accordance with U.S. law and American values related to privacy." We are pleased to provide you with our final report.

TIA was only one of the programs within DOD and elsewhere in the government involved, or with the potential for being involved, in data mining concerning U.S. persons. The committee believes that data mining plays a critical role in the fight against terrorism, but that it should be used—and can be effectively—only in ways that do not compromise the privacy of U.S. persons. That is the goal of our recommendations. We believe our recommendations both protect privacy and facilitate the appropriate, effective, and efficient use of data mining tools to fight terrorism.

While we have focused on DOD, we do not believe that all of the necessary safeguards are within the power of the Secretary of Defense. Some of our recommendations therefore encourage you to recommend to the President and Congress actions we believe are necessary to ensure meaningful privacy protection not only in DOD, but throughout the government. These recommendations are designed to create a consistent, government-wide standard to facilitate the sharing of information among agencies that is critical to fighting terrorism.

The committee's deliberations have been substantive, wide-ranging, and collegial. The committee is unanimous in most of its recommendations. A separate statement from William T. Coleman, Jr., reflecting his opposition to some of the committee's conclusions, is appended to our report. A separate statement from Floyd Abrams, which highlights why the committee disagrees with many of the views expressed in Mr. Coleman's statement, is also appended. Those statements and the seriousness of our discussions reflect the importance and difficulty of these issues.

The committee's work was greatly aided by the testimony of 60 witnesses from DOD, other government agencies, private industry, academia, and advocacy groups, and by extensive briefings for individual committee members and staff from many other individuals. These people are acknowledged individually in our report, but we wish to take this opportunity to thank them once again for their dedicated and selfless public service. Finally, I express my gratitude for the commitment, cooperation, and tireless work of the committee members; Lisa Davis, the committee's Executive Director and Designated Federal Official; and Professor Fred H. Cate, the committee's Reporter.

Yours sincerely,

Newton N. Minow

Newton N. Minow
Chairman

# Technology and Privacy Advisory Committee

Newton N. Minow
*Chairman*

Floyd Abrams
Zoë Baird
Griffin Bell
Gerhard Casper
William T. Coleman, Jr.
Lloyd N. Cutler
John O. Marsh, Jr.

Lisa A. Davis
*Executive Director and Designated Federal Official*

Fred H. Cate
*Reporter*

The document contains the executive summary and other selected material from TAPAC's final report. The complete report is available online on the committee's website at *www.sainc.com/TAPAC.*

# CONTENTS

## List of Abbreviations and Defined Terms

| | |
|---|---|
| ARDA | Advanced Research and Development Activity |
| "General Crimes Guidelines" | Attorney General's Guidelines on General Crimes, Racketeering Enterprise and Terrorism Enterprise Investigations |
| CAPPS II | Second generation Computer-Assisted Passenger Prescreening System, a TSA project |
| CIA | Central Intelligence Agency |
| DARPA | Defense Advanced Research Projects Agency |
| "Data Mining" | Searches of one or more electronic databases of information concerning U.S. persons, by or on behalf of an agency or employee of the government |
| DHS | Department of Homeland Security |
| DOD | Department of Defense |
| ECPA | Electronic Communications Privacy Act |
| FBI | Federal Bureau of Investigation |
| FISA | Foreign Intelligence Surveillance Act |
| FTC | Federal Trade Commission |
| GAO | General Accounting Office |
| IAO | Information Awareness Office, a former DARPA office |
| INS | Immigration and Naturalization Service |
| IT | Information technology |
| MATRIX | Multistate Anti-Terrorism Information Exchange |
| OECD | Organization for Economic Cooperation and Development |
| "OECD Guidelines" | Guidelines on the Protection of Privacy and Transborder Flows of Personal Data issued by the OECD Committee of Ministers in 1974 |
| OMB | Office of Management and Budget |
| SSNs | Social Security Numbers |
| TALON | Threat Alerts and Locally Observed Notices |
| TAPAC | Technology and Privacy Advisory Committee |
| TIA | Terrorism (formerly "Total") Information Awareness, a former DARPA project |
| TSA | Transportation Security Administration |
| "U.S. person" | Defined by Executive Order 12333 as an individual who is a U.S. citizen or permanent resident alien, a group or organization that is an unincorporated association substantially composed of U.S. citizens or permanent resident aliens, or a corporation incorporated in the United States (except if directed and controlled by a foreign government or governments). Because TAPAC is concerned only with the privacy interests of individuals, the report uses the term to refer only to a U.S. citizen or permanent resident alien. |
| USA PATRIOT Act | Uniting and Strengthening America by Providing Appropriate Tools Required to Intercept and Obstruct Terrorism Act |

# EXECUTIVE SUMMARY

*[Terrorism] poses extraordinary risks to our security, as well as to our constitutional freedoms, which could all too easily be compromised in the fight against this new and deadly terrorist threat.*

## TAPAC'S CREATION AND CHARGE

The United States faces, in the words of British Prime Minister Tony Blair, "a new and deadly virus."[1] That virus is "terrorism, whose intent to inflict destruction is unconstrained by human feeling and whose capacity to inflict it is enlarged by technology."[2]

As the murderous attacks of September 11 painfully demonstrated, this new threat is unlike anything the nation has faced before. The combination of coordinated, well-financed terrorists, willing to sacrifice their lives, potentially armed with weapons of mass destruction, capable of operating within our own borders poses extraordinary risks to our security, as well as to our constitutional freedoms, which could all too easily be compromised in the fight against this new and deadly terrorist threat.

To help guard against this, Secretary of Defense Donald Rumsfeld appointed the Technology and Privacy Advisory Committee ("TAPAC") in February 2003 to examine the use of "advanced information technologies to identify terrorists before they act."[3]

Secretary Rumsfeld charged the committee with developing safeguards "to ensure that the application of this or any like technology developed within [the Department of Defense] DOD is carried out in accordance with U.S. law and American values related to privacy."[4]*

The decision to create TAPAC was prompted by the escalating debate over the Terrorism Information Awareness ("TIA") program.† TIA had

* U.S. laws apply to surveillance, searches, and seizures of personally identifiable information conducted or authorized by government officials within the United States. Those laws apply outside of the United States only if the surveillance, search, or seizure involves a U.S. citizen (although not necessarily a permanent resident alien).

This report focuses exclusively on the privacy issues posed by U.S. government data mining programs under U.S. law to U.S. persons, which are defined under U.S. law as U.S. citizens and permanent resident aliens. It does not address data mining concerning federal government employees in connection with their employment.

† When first announced, the program was entitled "Total Information Awareness." The title was changed to "Terrorism Information Awareness" in May 2003.

*TIA was not unique in its potential for data mining. . . . [M]any other programs in use or under development . . . make similar uses of personal information concerning U.S. persons to detect and deter terrorist activities.*

been created by the Defense Advanced Research Projects Agency ("DARPA") in 2002 as a tool to "become much more efficient and more clever in the ways we find new sources of data, mine information from the new and old, generate information, make it available for analysis, convert it to knowledge, and create actionable options."[5]

TIA sparked controversy in Congress and the press, due in large part to the threat it was perceived as posing to informational privacy. On September 25, 2003, Congress terminated funding for the program with the exception of "processing, analysis, and collaboration tools for counter-terrorism foreign intelligence," specified in a classified annex to the Act. These tools may be used only in connection with "lawful military operations of the United States conducted outside the United States" or "lawful foreign intelligence activities conducted wholly overseas, or wholly against non-United States citizens."[6] This language makes clear that TIA-like activities may be continuing.

## THE SCOPE OF GOVERNMENT DATA MINING

TIA was not unique in its potential for data mining.* TAPAC is aware of many other programs in use or under development both within DOD and elsewhere in the government that make similar uses of personal information concerning U.S. persons to detect and deter terrorist activities, including:

- DOD programs to determine whether data mining can be used to identify individuals who pose a threat to U.S. forces abroad
- the intelligence community's Advanced Research and Development Activity center, based in the National Security Agency, to conduct "advanced research and development related to extracting intelligence from, and providing security for, information transmitted or manipulated by electronic means"[7]
- the Computer-Assisted Passenger Prescreening System in the Department of Homeland Security ("DHS")
- the Treasury Department's Financial Crimes Enforcement Network
- federally mandated "Know Your Customer" rules
- the "MATRIX" (Multistate Anti-Terrorism Information Exchange) system to link law enforcement records with other government and private-sector databases in eight states and DHS
- Congress' mandate in the Homeland Security Act that DHS "establish and utilize . . . a secure communications and information technology infrastructure, including data-mining and other advanced analytical tools," to "access, receive, and analyze data detect and identify threats of terrorism against the United States"[8]

## TAPAC'S CONCLUSIONS

After many public hearings, numerous background briefings, and extensive research, TAPAC has reached four broad conclusions:

**TIA was a flawed effort to achieve worthwhile ends.** It was flawed by its perceived insensitivity to

* We define "data mining" to mean: searches of one or more electronic databases of information concerning U.S. persons, by or on behalf of an agency or employee of the government.

*TIA was a flawed effort to achieve worthwhile ends. It was flawed by its perceived insensitivity to critical privacy issues, the manner in which it was presented to the public, and the lack of clarity and consistency with which it was described.*

critical privacy issues, the manner in which it was presented to the public, and the lack of clarity and consistency with which it was described. DARPA stumbled badly in its handling of TIA, for which the agency has paid a significant price in terms of its credibility in Congress and with the public. This comes at a time when DARPA's historically creative and ambitious research capacity is more necessary than ever. By maintaining its focus on imaginative, far-sighted research, at the same time that it takes account of informational privacy concerns, DARPA should rapidly regain its bearings. It is in the best interests of the nation for it to do so.

**Data mining is a vital tool in the fight against terrorism, but when used in connection with personal data concerning U.S. persons, data mining can present significant privacy issues.** Data mining tools, like most technologies, are inherently neutral: they can be used for good or ill. However, when those tools are used by the government to scrutinize personally identifiable data concerning U.S. persons who have done nothing to warrant suspicion, if they are conducted without an adequate predicate they run the risk of becoming the 21st-century equivalent of general searches, which the authors of the Bill of Rights were so concerned to protect against.

To be certain, data mining has many valuable and lawful uses in both the private and public sectors. In many settings it may prove less intrusive to privacy than other techniques for guarding against terrorist threats. Moreover, the same technologies that make data mining feasible can be used to reduce the amount of personally identifiable data necessary, facilitate data mining with anonymized data, and create immutable audit trails and other protections against misuse.

However, when data mining involves the government accessing personally identifiable information about U.S. persons, it also raises privacy issues. The magnitude of those issues varies depending upon many factors, including: the sensitivity of the data being mined, the expectation of privacy reasonably associated with the data, the consequences of an individual being identified by an inquiry, and the number (or percentage) of U.S. persons identified in response to an inquiry who have not otherwise done anything to warrant government suspicion.

**In developing and using data mining tools the government can and must protect privacy.** This has never been more starkly presented than following the September 11 terrorist attacks, which vividly demonstrated the need to deploy the tools

*Data mining is a vital tool in the fight against terrorism, but when used in connection with personal data concerning U.S. persons, data mining can present significant privacy issues.*

necessary to protect and defend the nation without violating our constitutional values in the process.

Striking a balance between security and privacy is no easy task. Alexander Hamilton wrote in Federalist Paper 8 in 1787 that "[s]afety from external danger is the most powerful director of national conduct. Even the ardent love of liberty will, after a time, give way to its dictates." "To be more safe," he concluded, nations "at length become willing to run the risk of being less free."[9] The Supreme Court wrote in 1963 that it is "under the pressing exigencies of crisis, that there is the greatest temptation to dispense with fundamental constitutional guarantees which, it is feared, will inhibit governmental action."[10]

This is precisely the challenge our nation faces today, a challenge made immediate and critical by the magnitude of the terrorist threat, its sustained nature, and the fact that it comes not from an identified enemy abroad but from a largely invisible enemy that may be operating within our borders.

Existing legal requirements applicable to the government's many data mining programs are numerous, but disjointed and often outdated, and as a result may compromise the protection

## Data Mining Checklist

*The Existence and Purpose of Data Mining*

1 Is the proposed activity or system likely to involve the acquisition, use, or sharing of personally identifiable information about U.S. persons?

2 What purpose(s) does the data mining serve? Is it lawful? Is it within the agency's authority? Is it sufficiently important to warrant the risks to informational privacy that data mining poses?

3 Is data mining necessary to accomplish that purpose—i.e., could the purpose be accomplished as well without data mining?

4 Is the data mining tool designed to access, use, retain, and disseminate the least data necessary to serve the purposes for which it is intended?

5 Is the data mining tool designed to use anonymized data whenever possible?

*Data Mining Personally Identifiable Information*

6 Are there specific and articulable facts that data mining personally identifiable information (or reidentifying previously anonymized information) concerning U.S. persons will be conducted in a manner that otherwise complies with the requirements of applicable laws and recommendations; is reasonably related to identifying or apprehending terrorists, preventing terrorist attacks, or locating or preventing the use of weapons of mass destruction; is likely to yield information relevant to national security; and is not practicable with anonymized data?

*The Sources and Nature of Data Concerning U.S. Persons*

7 Are the data appropriate for their intended use, taking into account the purpose(s) for which the data were collected, their age, and the conditions under which they have been stored and protected?

8 Are data being accessed or acquired from third parties in violation of the terms and conditions (usually reflected in a privacy policy) under which they were collected?

9 If data are being acquired directly from data subjects, have the individuals been provided with appropriate notice, consistent with the purpose of the data mining activity?

*Existing legal requirements applicable to the government's many data mining programs . . . may compromise the protection of privacy, public confidence, and the nation's ability to craft effective and lawful responses to terrorism.*

of privacy, public confidence, and the nation's ability to craft effective and lawful responses to terrorism. This is especially true in the setting on which TAPAC focused—analyzing personally identifiable data to protect against terrorist threats.

The legal protections that have historically applied in this context recognize distinctions between U.S. persons and non-U.S. persons, and between law enforcement and national security, and between activities that take place in the United States as

10 Are data being sought in the order provided by Executive Order 12333—i.e., from or with the consent of the data subject, from publicly available sources, from proprietary sources, through a method requiring authorization less than probable cause (e.g., a pen register or trap and trace device), through a method requiring a warrant, and finally through a method requiring a wiretap order?

11 Are personally identifiable data being left in place whenever possible? If such data are being acquired or transferred, is there a system in place for ensuring that they are returned or destroyed as soon as practicable?

***The Impact of Data Mining***

12 What are the likely effect(s) on individuals identified through the data mining—i.e., will they be the subject of further investigation or will they be immediately subject to some adverse action?

13 Does the data mining tool yield a rate of false positives that is acceptable in view of the purpose of the search, the severity of the effect of being identified, and the likelihood of further investigation?

14 Is there an appropriate system in place for dealing with false positives (e.g., reporting false positives to developers to improve the system, correcting incorrect information if possible, etc.), including identifying the frequency and effects of false positives?

***Oversight of Data Mining***

15 Are data secured against accidental or deliberate unauthorized access, use, alteration, or destruction, and access to the data mining tool restricted to persons with a legitimate need and protected by appropriate access controls taking into account the sensitivity of the data?

16 Does the data mining tool generate, to the extent technologically possible, an immutable audit trail showing which data have been accessed or transferred, by what users, and for what purposes?

17 Will the data mining tool be subject to continual oversight to ensure that it is used appropriately and lawfully, and that informational privacy issues raised by new developments or discoveries are identified and addressed promptly?

18 Are all persons engaged in developing or using data mining tools trained in their appropriate use and the laws and regulations applicable to their use?

19 Have determinations as to the efficacy and appropriateness of data mining been made or reviewed by an official other than those intimately involved with the development, acquisition, or use of the data mining tool?

*Clear, uniform laws and standards governing data mining are necessary . . .*
*to use data mining tools effectively and aggressively in the fight against terrorism.*

opposed to those that take place beyond our borders. This "line at the border" approach to privacy law and to national security is now increasingly inadequate because of the new threat from terrorists who may be operating within our borders, and advances in digital technologies, including the Internet, that have exponentially increased the volume of data available about individuals and greatly reduced the financial and other obstacles to retaining, sharing, and transferring those data across borders. These developments highlight the need for new regulatory boundaries to help protect civil liberties and national security at the same time. It is time to update the law to respond to new challenges.

The stakes could not be higher. Clear, uniform laws and standards governing data mining are necessary to empower DOD and other government agencies to use data mining tools effectively and aggressively in the fight against terrorism. Those laws and standards are also necessary to protect informational privacy, which is both important in its own right and is often critical to a range of fundamental civil liberties, including our rights to speak, protest, associate, worship, and participate in the political process free from government intrusion or intimidation.

## Recommendations Concerning DOD Data Mining

We believe it is possible to use information technologies to protect national security without compromising the privacy of U.S. persons. The answer lies in clear rules and policy guidance, adopted through an open and credible political process, supplemented with educational and technological tools, developed as an integral part of the technologies that threaten privacy, and enforced through appropriate managerial, political, and judicial oversight.

### Recommendation 1

**DOD should safeguard the privacy of U.S. persons when using data mining to fight terrorism.**

### Recommendation 2

**The Secretary should establish a regulatory framework applicable to all data mining conducted by, or under the authority of, DOD, known or reasonably likely to involve personally identifiable information concerning U.S. persons.** The essential elements of that framework include a written finding by agency heads authorizing data mining; minimum technical requirements for data mining systems (including data minimization, data anonymization, creation of an audit trail, security and access controls, and training for personnel involved in data mining); special protections for data mining involving databases from other government agencies or from private industry; authorization from the Foreign Intelligence Surveillance Court before engaging in data mining with personally identifiable information concerning U.S. persons or reidentifying previously anonymized information concerning U.S. persons; and regular audits to ensure compliance.

We recommend *excluding* from these requirements data mining that is limited to foreign intelligence that does not involve U.S. persons; data mining concerning federal government employees in connection with their employment; and data mining that is based on particularized suspicion, including searches to identify or locate a specific individual (e.g., a suspected terrorist) from airline or cruise ship passenger manifests or other lists of names or other nonsensitive information about U.S. persons.

## Summary of TAPAC Recommendations

*Recommendations Concerning DOD Data Mining*

### RECOMMENDATION 1

DOD should safeguard the privacy of U.S. persons when using data mining to fight terrorism. "Data mining" is defined to mean: searches of one or more electronic databases of information concerning U.S. persons, by or on behalf of an agency or employee of the government.

### RECOMMENDATION 2

The Secretary should establish a regulatory framework applicable to all data mining conducted by, or under the authority of, DOD, known or reasonably likely to involve personally identifiable information concerning U.S. persons. The requirements of this section apply to all DOD programs involving data mining concerning U.S. persons, with three exceptions: data mining (1) based on particularized suspicion, including searches of passenger manifests and similar lists; (2) that is limited to foreign intelligence that does not involve U.S. persons; or (3) that concerns federal government employees in connection with their employment. Data mining that is limited to information that is routinely available without charge or subscription to the public—on the Internet, in telephone directories, or in public records to the extent authorized by law—should be conditioned only on the written authorization described in Recommendation 2.1 and the compliance audits described in Recommendation 2.5. All other data mining concerning U.S. persons should comply with all of the following requirements:

### RECOMMENDATION 2.1

Written finding by agency head authorizing data mining. Before an agency can employ data mining known or reasonably likely to involve data concerning U.S. persons, the agency head should first make a written finding that complies with the requirements of this recommendation authorizing the data mining.

An agency head may make the written finding described above either for programs that include data mining as one element, and data mining concerning U.S. persons may occur, or for specific applications of data mining where the use of information known or likely to concern U.S. persons is clearly anticipated.

### RECOMMENDATION 2.2

Technical requirements for data mining. Data mining of databases known or reasonably likely to include personally identifiable information about U.S. persons should employ or be subject to the requirements of this recommendation (i.e., data minimization, data anonymization, audit trail, security and access, and training).

### RECOMMENDATION 2.3

Third-party databases. Data mining involving databases from other government agencies or from private industry may present special risks. Such data mining involving, or reasonably likely to involve, U.S. persons, should adhere to the principles set forth in this recommendation.

### RECOMMENDATION 2.4

Personally identifiable information. It is not always possible to engage in data mining using anonymized data. Moreover, even searches involving anonymized data will ultimately result in matches which must be reidentified using personally identifiable information. The use of personally identifiable information known or reasonably likely to concern U.S. persons in data mining should adhere to the following provisions:

An agency within DOD may engage in data mining using personally identifiable information known or reasonably likely to concern U.S. persons on the condition that, prior to the commencement of the search, DOD obtains from the Foreign Intelligence Surveillance Court a written order authorizing the search based on the existence of specific and articulable facts that meet the requirements of this recommendation.

DOD may seek the approval from the Foreign Intelligence Surveillance Court either for programs that include data mining as one element, and data mining of personally identifiable information known or likely to include information on U.S. persons may arise, or for specific applications of data mining where the use of personally identifiable information known or likely to include information on U.S. persons is clearly anticipated.

An agency may reidentify previously anonymized data known or reasonably likely to concern a U.S. person on the condition that DOD obtains from the Foreign Intelligence Surveillance Court a written order authorizing the reidentification based on the existence of specific and articulable facts that meet the requirements of this recommendation.

Without obtaining a court order, the government may, in exigent circumstances, search personally identifiable information or reidentify anonymized information obtained through data mining if it meets the requirements of this recommendation.

**RECOMMENDATION 2.5**
Auditing for compliance. Any program or activity that involves data mining known or reasonably likely to include personally identifiable information about U.S. persons should be audited not less than annually to ensure compliance with the provisions of this recommendation and other applicable laws and regulations.

**RECOMMENDATION 3**
DOD should, to the extent permitted by law, support research into means for improving the accuracy and effectiveness of data mining systems and technologies, technological and other tools for enhancing privacy protection, and the broader legal, ethical, social, and practical issues in connection with data mining concerning U.S. persons.

**RECOMMENDATION 4**
The Secretary should create a policy-level privacy officer.

**RECOMMENDATION 5**
The Secretary should create a panel of external advisors to advise the Secretary, the privacy officer, and other DOD officials on identifying and resolving informational privacy issues, and on the development and implementation of appropriate privacy protection mechanisms.

**RECOMMENDATION 6**
The Secretary should create and ensure the effective operation of meaningful oversight mechanisms.

**RECOMMENDATION 7**
The Secretary should work to develop a culture of sensitivity to, and knowledge about, privacy issues involving U.S. persons throughout DOD's research, acquisition, and operational activities.

***Recommendations Concerning Government Data Mining***

**RECOMMENDATION 8**
The Secretary should recommend that Congress and the President establish one framework of legal, technological, training, and oversight mechanisms necessary to guarantee the privacy of U.S. persons in the context of national security and law enforcement activities.

**RECOMMENDATION 9**
The Secretary should recommend that the President appoint an inter-agency committee to help ensure the quality and consistency of federal government efforts to safeguard informational privacy in the context of national security and law enforcement activities.

**RECOMMENDATION 10**
The Secretary should recommend that the President appoint a panel of external advisors to advise the President concerning federal government efforts to safeguard informational privacy in the context of national security and law enforcement activities.

**RECOMMENDATION 11**
The Secretary should recommend that the President and Congress take those steps necessary to ensure the protection of U.S. persons' privacy and the efficient and effective oversight of government data mining activities through the judiciary and by this nation's elected leaders through a politically credible process. Specifically, Congress and the President should authorize the Foreign Intelligence Surveillance Court to receive requests for orders under Recommendations 2.4 and 8 and to grant or deny such orders, and each house of Congress should identify a single committee to receive all of the agencies' reports concerning data mining.

**RECOMMENDATION 12**
The Secretary should recommend that the President and Congress support research into means for improving the accuracy and effectiveness of data mining systems and technologies; technological and other tools for enhancing privacy protection; and the broader legal, ethical, social, and practical issues involved with data mining concerning U.S. persons.

In addition, we recommend that data mining that is limited to information that is routinely available without charge or subscription to the public—on the Internet, in telephone directories, or in public records to the extent authorized by law—should be subject to only the requirements that it be conducted pursuant to the written authorization of the agency head (as specified in Recommendation 2.1) and auditing for compliance (as specified in Recommendation 2.5).

**RECOMMENDATION 3**

**DOD should, to the extent permitted by law, support research into means for improving the accuracy and effectiveness of data mining systems and technologies, technological and other tools for enhancing privacy protection, and the broader legal, ethical, social, and practical issues in connection with data mining concerning U.S. persons.**

**RECOMMENDATION 4**

**The Secretary should create a policy-level privacy officer.**

**RECOMMENDATION 5**

**The Secretary should create a panel of external advisors to advise the Secretary, the privacy officer, and other DOD officials on identifying and resolving informational privacy issues, and on the development and implementation of appropriate privacy protection mechanisms.**

**RECOMMENDATION 6**

**The Secretary should create and ensure the effective operation of meaningful oversight mechanisms.**

**RECOMMENDATION 7**

**The Secretary should work to ensure a culture of sensitivity to, and knowledge about, privacy issues involving U.S. persons throughout DOD and all of its research, acquisition, and operational activities.** To aid the Secretary in this important task we offer a checklist of questions as a useful guide for identifying specific informational privacy issues related to data mining.

## RECOMMENDATIONS CONCERNING GOVERNMENT DATA MINING

While TAPAC focused on TIA and related DARPA programs, it is counterproductive to the protection of both privacy and national security to address only these, while ignoring the many other government programs that use personal information on U.S. persons. Moreover, the privacy issues presented by data mining cannot be resolved by DOD alone. Action by Congress, the President, and the courts is necessary as well. Finally, because DOD is the only federal department to have an external advisory committee to examine the privacy implications of its programs, TAPAC occupies a unique position. We therefore direct our recommendations to the broad range of government data mining activities.

**RECOMMENDATION 8**

**The Secretary should recommend that Congress and the President establish one framework of legal, technological, training, and oversight mechanisms necessary to guarantee the privacy of U.S. persons in the context of national security and law enforcement activities.** A government-wide approach is desirable to address the significant

*While TAPAC focused on TIA and related DARPA programs, it is counterproductive to the protection of both privacy and national security to address only these, . . . ignoring the many other government programs that use personal information.*

privacy issues raised by the many programs under development, or already in operation, that involve the use of personally identifiable information concerning U.S. persons for national security and law enforcement purposes.

We therefore believe that the provisions of Recommendation 2, which concern DOD's programs that involve data mining, should also be implemented across the federal government and made applicable to all government departments and agencies that develop, acquire, or use data mining tools in connection with U.S. persons for national security or law enforcement purposes.

We do not suggest that the resolution of informational privacy issues will be the same in every setting. Clearly, some modifications will be necessary. We believe, however, that government efforts to protect national security and fight crime and to protect privacy will be enhanced by the articulation of government-wide principles and a consistent system of laws and processes. National standards will also help provide clear models for state and local government efforts as well.

#### RECOMMENDATION 9

**The Secretary should recommend that the President appoint an inter-agency committee to help ensure the quality and consistency of federal government efforts to safeguard informational privacy in the context of national security and law enforcement activities.**

#### RECOMMENDATION 10

**The Secretary should recommend that the President appoint a panel of external advisors to advise the President concerning federal government efforts to safeguard informational privacy in the context of national security and law enforcement activities.**

#### RECOMMENDATION 11

**The Secretary should recommend that the President and Congress take those steps necessary to ensure the protection of U.S. persons' privacy and the efficient and effective oversight of government data mining activities through the judiciary and by this nation's elected leaders through a politically credible process.** This includes adopting new, consistent protections, along the lines of these recommendations, for information privacy in the law enforcement and national security contexts. **In addition, we believe Congress and the President should work together to enact the legislation necessary to authorize the Foreign Intelligence Surveillance Court to receive requests for orders under Recommendations 2 and 8 and to grant or deny such orders.**

There is also a critical need for Congress to exercise appropriate oversight, especially given the fact that many data mining programs may involve classified information which would prevent immediate public disclosure. We believe that each house of Congress should identify a single committee to exercise oversight of data mining activities, and that each agency's privacy officer and agency head should report jointly to those committees at least annually.

#### RECOMMENDATION 12

**The Secretary should recommend that the President and Congress support research into means for improving the accuracy and effectiveness of data mining systems and technologies; technological and other tools for enhancing privacy protection; and the broader legal, ethical, social, and practical issues involved with data mining concerning U.S. persons.**

## Impact of TAPAC Recommendations on Government Data Mining

*(i.e., searches of one or more electronic databases of information concerning U.S. persons, by or on behalf of an agency or employee of the government)*

| Type of Information | New Recommended Requirements |
|---|---|
| Data mining that is not known or reasonably likely to involve *personally identifiable* information about *U.S. persons* (i.e., U.S. citizens and permanent residents) | No new requirements |
| Data mining limited to *foreign intelligence* that does not concern U.S. *persons.* | No new requirements |
| Data mining known or reasonably likely to involve *personally identifiable* information about U.S. *persons:* | |
| • If based on *particularized suspicion* about a specific individual, including searches to identify or locate a specific individual (e.g., a suspected terrorist) from airline or cruise ship *passenger manifests* or other lists of names or other nonsensitive information about U.S. persons. | No new requirements |
| • If concerning *federal government employees* that is solely in connection with their employment. | No new requirements |
| • If limited to searches of information that is *routinely available without charge or subscription to the public*—on the Internet, in telephone directories, or in public records to the extent authorized by law. | 1 Administrative authorization (set forth in Recommendation 2.1), which may be granted on a "per program" or "per search" basis; and<br>2 Regular compliance audits (set forth in Recommendation 2.5). |
| • If conducted with *deidentified data* (i.e., data from which personally identifying elements such as name or Social Security Number have been removed or obscured). | All new requirements apply (i.e., administrative authorization, compliance with technical requirements, special rules for third-party databases, and regular compliance audits, as set forth in Recommendations 2.1, 2.2, 2.3, and 2.5), *except for* need to obtain a Foreign Intelligence Surveillance Court order (set forth in Recommendation 2.4). |
| • If conducted with *personally identifiable information.* | All new requirements apply (as set forth in Recommendations 2.1-2.5), *including* application to the Foreign Intelligence Surveillance Court (Recommendation 2.4), which can be made on a "per program" or "per search" basis. |

*Our goal in these recommendations is to articulate a framework of law and technology to enable the government simultaneously to combat terrorism and safeguard privacy.*

## Conclusion

Our goal in these recommendations is to articulate a framework of law and technology to enable the government simultaneously to combat terrorism and safeguard privacy. We believe rapid action is necessary to address the host of government programs that involve data mining concerning U.S. persons and to provide clear direction to the people responsible for developing, procuring, implementing, and overseeing those programs.

While these recommendations impose additional burdens on government officials before they employ some data mining tools, we believe that in the long-run they will enhance not only informational privacy, but national security as well. They are designed to help break down the barriers to information-sharing among agencies that have previously hampered national security efforts, to provide sufficient clarity concerning access to and use of personal information concerning U.S. persons so that DOD and other government officials can use such information appropriately, and to ensure that scarce national security resources are deployed strategically and effectively.

This broader, more comprehensive approach is essential if our nation is to achieve its goal of combating terrorism *and* safeguarding the privacy of U.S. persons. We must not sacrifice liberty for security, because as Benjamin Franklin warned more than two centuries ago, "they that can give up essential liberty to purchase a little temporary safety deserve neither liberty nor safety."[11] Franklin might well have added that those who trade liberty for safety all too often achieve neither.

## Notes

1 Tony Blair, Address before a Joint Session of Congress, Washington, DC, July 17, 2003.

2 Id.

3 U.S. Department of Defense, Technology and Privacy Advisory Committee Charter (Mar. 25, 2003).

4 Id.

5 John Poindexter, Overview of the Information Awareness Office, prepared remarks for delivery at DARPATech 2002, Anaheim, CA, Aug. 2, 2002, at 1.

6 Department of Defense Appropriations Act, 2004, Pub. L. No. 108-84, § 8183 (Sept. 25, 2003).

7 Memo from CIA Director George Tenet (May 11, 1998).

8 Homeland Security Act of 2002, Pub. L. No. 107-296, §§ 201(d)(1), (d)(14) (Nov. 25, 2002).

9 Alexander Hamilton, "The Consequences of Hostilities Between the States" (Federalist Paper 8), *New York Packet*, Nov. 20, 1787.

10 Kennedy v. Mendoza-Martinez, 372 U.S. 144, 165 (1963).

11 Benjamin Franklin, *Historical Review of Pennsylvania* 1 (1759).

# Appendix A Biographies of Technology and Privacy Advisory Committee Members and Staff

## TAPAC Members

**Newton N. Minow, Chairman,** is Senior Counsel to the law firm of Sidley Austin Brown & Wood. He was a managing partner with Sidley & Austin from 1965–1991. He served as a U.S. Army Sergeant in the China-Burma India Theater in World War II. He served as a Law Clerk to the Honorable Fred M. Vinson, Chief Justice of the United States, and as Assistant Counsel to Governor Adlai E. Stevenson. In 1961, President John F. Kennedy appointed him Chairman of the Federal Communications Commission. Mr. Minow has served as Chairman of the Carnegie Corporation, the Public Broadcasting Service, and The RAND Corporation, and as a trustee of the Mayo Clinic. He is a life trustee of Northwestern University and the University of Notre Dame. He co-chaired the 1976 and 1980 presidential debates and is Vice Chairman of the Commission on Presidential Debates, which sponsors the debates. He has served on numerous presidential commissions. A graduate of Northwestern University, he is the Walter Annenberg Professor Emeritus there, as well as the author of four books and numerous professional journal and magazine articles and the recipient of 12 honorary degrees.

**Floyd Abrams** is a partner in the New York law firm of Cahill Gordon & Reindel LLP and is the William J. Brennan, Jr. Visiting Professor of First Amendment Law at the Columbia Graduate School of Journalism. Mr. Abrams has argued frequently in the Supreme Court in a large number of its most significant First Amendment cases. He graduated from Cornell University in 1956 and the Yale Law School in 1960. He was a Visiting Lecturer at the Yale Law School from 1974 to 1980 and 1986 to 1989 and the Columbia Law School from 1981 to 1985. He is a recipient of the William J. Brennan, Jr. Award for outstanding contribution to public discourse; the Learned Hand Award of the American Jewish Committee; the Thurgood Marshall Award of the Association of the Bar of the City of New York; the New York Press Club John Peter Zenger Award; the Judge Louis J. Capozzoli Award of the New York County Lawyers Association; the Democracy Award of the Radio Television News Directors Foundation; Ross Essay Prize of the American Bar Association; and many others. Mr. Abrams was Chairman of the Communications Committee of the Association of the Bar of the City of New York, the Committee on Freedom of Speech and of the Press of the Individual Rights Section of the American Bar Association; the Committee of the Freedom of Expression of the Litigation Section of the American Bar Association; and of Mayor Edward Koch's Committee on Appointments. He currently chairs the New York State Commission on Public Access to Court Records.

**Zoë Baird** is president of the Markle Foundation, a private philanthropy that focuses on using information and communications technologies ("IT") to address critical public needs, particularly in the areas of health care and national security. Since joining the Foundation in 1998, Ms. Baird has developed it into an operating foundation that, in addition to its work in health care and national security, has been instrumental in working with the governments of the G-8 countries and major developing countries to establish mechanisms to address international IT policy and to enable the use of IT to achieve development goals. Ms. Baird's career spans business, government and academia. She has been senior vice president and general counsel of Aetna, Inc., a senior visiting scholar at Yale Law School, counselor and staff executive at General Electric, and a partner in the law firm of O'Melveny & Myers. She was Associate Counsel to President Jimmy Carter and an attorney in the Office of Legal Counsel of the U.S. Department of Justice. She served on President Clinton's Foreign Intelligence Advisory Board and on the International Competition Policy Advisory Committee to the Attorney General. Ms. Baird is a member of the American Law Institute and served on the congressional Commission on the Roles and Missions of the Intelligence Community. She serves on a number of private and non-profit boards of directors.

**Griffin Bell** joined King & Spalding as a partner in 1953 and became Managing Partner in 1958. In 1961, President John F. Kennedy appointed him to serve as a United States Circuit Judge on the Fifth Circuit Court of Appeals. He served as the 72nd Attorney General of the United States from 1977-79. He is a member of the American College of Trial Lawyers, serving as its President from 1985–86. He is also a member of the American Law Institute. Judge Bell was the initial Chairman of the Atlanta Commission on Crime and Juvenile Delinquency. During 1980, he headed the American delegation to the conference on Security and Cooperation in Europe, held in Madrid. In 1984, Judge Bell received the Thomas Jefferson Memorial Foundation Award for Excellence in Law. From 1985-87, Judge Bell served on the Secretary of State's Advisory Committee on South Africa, and in 1989, he was appointed Vice Chairman of President Bush's Commission on Federal Ethics Law Reform. During the Iran Contra investigation, he was counsel to President Bush. Judge Bell graduated *cum laude* from Mercer University Law School in 1948.

**Gerhard Casper** is President Emeritus of Stanford University and the Peter and Helen Bing Professor in Undergraduate Education at Stanford. He is also a Professor of Law, a Senior Fellow at the Institute for International Studies, and a Professor of Political Science (by courtesy). Professor Casper studied law at the universities of Freiburg and Hamburg, where, in 1961, he earned his first law degree. He attended Yale Law School, obtaining his Master of Laws degree in 1962. He then returned to Freiburg, where he received his doctorate in 1964. He has been awarded honorary doctorates, most recently in law from Yale and in philosophy from Uppsala. In the fall of 1964, Professor Casper immigrated to the United States, spending two years as Assistant Professor of Political Science at the University of California at Berkeley. In 1966, he joined the faculty of the University of Chicago Law School, and between 1979 and 1987 served as Dean of the Law School. In 1989, he was appointed Provost of the University of Chicago. He served as President of Stanford University from 1992–2000. Professor Casper is the author of numerous scholarly books and articles and occasional pieces. From 1977 to 1991, he was an editor of *The Supreme Court Review*. He has been elected to membership in the American Law Institute (1977), the International Academy of Comparative Law, the American Academy of Arts and Sciences (1980), the Order pour le mérite für Wissenschaften und Künste (Order pour le mérite for the Sciences and Arts) (1993), and the American Philosophical Society (1996). Professor Casper serves as a successor trustee of Yale University, a member of the Board of Trustees of the Central European University in Budapest, and a member of the Trilateral Commission. He is also a member of various additional boards, including the Council of the American Law Institute and the Board of the American Academy in Berlin.

**William T. Coleman, Jr.** is a Senior Partner and the Senior Counselor in the law firm of O'Melveny and Myers. He received his A.B. *summa cum laude* from the University of Pennsylvania and his LL.B. *magna cum laude* from Harvard University, where he was an editor of the *Harvard Law Review*. He clerked for the Honorable Herbert F. Goodrich on the U.S. Court of Appeals for the Third Circuit, and for the Honorable Felix Frankfurter on the U.S. Supreme Court. He was Secretary of the Department of Transportation during the Ford Administration. He is a member of the Executive Committee of the Trilateral Commission, the Council on Foreign Relations, and the Boards of Trustees of the Carnegie Institution of Washington, the Brookings Institution, the Philadelphia Museum of Art (Vice President), and the New York City Ballet, Inc. He was a member of the Board of Directors of the National Symphony Orchestra, a Trustee of the National Gallery of Art, and an Advisory Director of the Metropolitan Opera. He is a former member of the Board of Overseers of Harvard University and of the Boards of Directors of AMAX, Chase Manhattan Bank, N.A., Chase Manhattan Corporation, CIGNA Corporation, IBM Corporation, Pan American World Airways, PepsiCo., Inc., Philadelphia Electric Company, and New American Holdings. He is the author of many scholarly articles and a fellow of the American College of Trial Lawyers, the American Academy of Appellate Lawyers, of the American Law Institute, the American Academy of Arts and Sciences, and of the American Philosophical Association. He served as President and as Chair of the NAACP Legal Defense and Educational Fund. Mr. Coleman has received the French Legion of Honor and the Presidential Medal of Freedom.

**Lloyd N. Cutler** is a founding partner of the law firm of Wilmer, Cutler & Pickering. He served as Counsel to Presidents Clinton and Carter; Special Counsel to the President on Ratification of the Salt II Treaty (1979–1980); the President's Special Representative for Maritime Resource and Boundary Negotiations with Canada (1977–1979); and Senior Consultant, President's Commission on Strategic Forces (Scowcroft Commission, 1983–1984). He was a member and former Chairman of the Quadrennial Commission on Legislative, Executive and Judicial Salaries, and was a member of the President's Commission on Federal Ethics Law Reform (1989). Mr. Cutler is a graduate of Yale University (B.A. 1936; LL.B. 1939) and was awarded a Yale honorary Doctor of Laws degree in 1983. He also was awarded an honorary Doctor of Laws degree from Princeton University in 1994; the Jefferson Medal in Law at the University of Virginia in 1995; the Fordham-Stein Prize, Fordham University School of Law, 1995; and the Marshall-Wythe medal of the Law School of William and Mary. Mr. Cutler was a founder and Co-Chairman of the Lawyers Committee on Civil Rights Under Law. He has served as Chairman of the Board of the Salzburg Seminar; Co-Chairman of the Committee on the Constitutional System; a member of the Council of the American Law Institute; a trustee emeritus of The Brookings Institution and a member of its Executive Committee; and an Honorary Bencher of the Middle Temple. He also has served as a director of a number of national business corporations.

**John O. Marsh, Jr.** is a Distinguished Professor of Law at George Mason University, concentrating on cyberterrorism and national security law. He enlisted in the U.S. Army in 1944 and was commissioned a second lieutenant at age 19. He later served in the Army Reserve and the Virginia National Guard, much of his service being in the 116th Infantry Regiment. He graduated from the Army Airborne and Jumpmaster Schools and earned Senior Parachutist Wings. He received his law degree in 1951 from Washington and Lee University and began his practice of law in Strasburg, VA. He was elected to four terms in Congress from the Seventh District of Virginia (1963–71), and served on the House Appropriations Committee. Choosing not to seek a fifth term, he resumed the practice of law. In March 1973, he returned to federal service as Assistant Secretary of Defense for

Legislative Affairs. In January 1974, he became Assistant for National Security Affairs to Vice President Ford, and in August 1974 became Counselor, with Cabinet rank, to President Ford. He chaired the Presidential Committee for the Reorganization of the U.S. Intelligence Community in 1975–76. From 1981–1989, he served as Secretary of the Army; his tenure was the longest of any Secretary in American history. Secretary Marsh has been awarded the Department of Defense Distinguished Public Service Award on six occasions, has been decorated by the governments of France and Brazil, and holds the Presidential Citizens Medal. He was selected as Virginian of the Year for 1990 by the Virginia Press Association and has received the George Catlett Marshall Medal for public service from the Association of the United States Army. He is a member of the advisory council of the Virginia Institute of Marine Science, chairs the advisory committee of Virginia Inland Port, and is a member of the Special Congressional Panel on Terrorism to Assess Federal, State and Local Response to Weapons of Mass Destruction (the Gilmore Commission).

## Executive Director and Designated Federal Official

**Lisa A. Davis** serves as the Executive Director and Designated Federal Official of the Technology and Privacy Advisory Committee. Mrs. Davis was appointed Principal Assistant Deputy Under Secretary of Defense for Industrial Policy on December 3, 2001. Her responsibilities include world-wide industrial base management initiatives, such as E-business solutions, acquisition management improvements, and best business practices. She brings to this position extensive experience in defense contracting and acquisition policy, management, and legislation from positions in the Defense Department, industry, and Capitol Hill. She has negotiated and managed major systems acquisitions for the Army, Navy, and Marine Corps, and has held positions of increasing responsibility in the office of the Secretary of Defense. Mrs. Davis graduated with honors from Ball State University, and earned the title Certified Contracts Manager from the National Contract Management Association/Defense Systems Management College.

## Reporter

**Fred H. Cate** is the reporter for TAPAC. He is a Distinguished Professor and director of the Center for Applied Cybersecurity Research at Indiana University. He appears regularly before Congress, government agencies, and professional and industry groups on privacy, security, and other information law matters. Professor Cate directed the Electronic Information Privacy and Commerce Study for the Brookings Institution, chaired the International Telecommunication Union's High-Level Experts on Electronic Signatures and Certification Authorities, and was a member of the Federal Trade Commission's Advisory Committee on Online Access and Security. He is a senior policy advisor to the Center for Information Policy Leadership at Hunton & Williams, a member of Microsoft's Trustworthy Computing Academic Advisory Board, and a member of the board of editors of *Privacy & Information Law Report*. He has led projects for the American Enterprise Institute, The Annenberg Washington Program, and the Brookings Institution. He is the author of many articles and books, including *Privacy in the Information Age*, *Privacy in Perspective*, and *The Internet and the First Amendment*. A member of the American Law Institute and a Senator and Fellow of the Phi Beta Kappa Society, he received his J.D. and his A.B. with Honors and Distinction from Stanford University.

# APPENDIX B TAPAC WITNESSES

**The Hon. E.C. Aldridge**, Under Secretary of Defense (Acquisition, Technology and Logistics)

**Lieutenant General Keith B. Alexander**, Deputy Chief of Staff for Intelligence, U.S. Army

**Stewart Aly**, Associate Deputy General Counsel, Department of Defense

**Maureen Baginski**, Executive Assistant Director of Intelligence, Federal Bureau of Investigation

**Stewart Baker**, Attorney at Law, Steptoe and Johnson, LLP

**Jennifer Barrett**, Chief Privacy Officer, Acxiom

**Jerry Berman**, President, Center for Democracy and Technology

**John Brennan**, Director, Terrorist Threat Integration Center

**Scott Charney**, Chief Trustworthy Computing Strategist, Microsoft Corp.

**Gary Clayton**, Founder and CEO, Privacy Council, Inc.

**William P. Crowell**

**Michael de Janes**, General Counsel and Secretary, ChoicePoint

**Robert L. Deitz**, Deputy General Counsel (Intelligence), Department of Defense

**Jim Dempsey**, Executive Director, Center for Democracy and Technology

**Viet Dinh**, Professor of Law, Georgetown University Law Center

**Brigadier General George R. Fay**, Commanding General, U.S. Army Intelligence & Security Command

**Dr. Usama Fayyad**, President, DMX Group; Chairman, Revenue Science, Inc.

**Dr. Edward W. Felten**, Professor of Computer Science and Director of the Secure Internet Programming Laboratory, Princeton University; Co-Chairman of DARPA Information Science and Technology Advisory Board

**Dan Gallington**, Senior Research Fellow at the Potomac Institute for Policy Studies

**The Hon. Governor James S. Gilmore, III**, Chair, Congressional Advisory Panel to Assess Domestic Response Capabilities for Terrorism Involving Weapons of Mass Destruction

**Jamie Gorelick**, Partner, Wilmer, Cutler & Pickering

**Jeff Green**, Senior Attorney, Standards of Conduct Office, Department of Defense

**Carol Haave**, Deputy Under Secretary of Defense (Security and Information Operations)

**Dr. David Jensen**, Research Assistant Professor of Computer Science and Director of the Knowledge Discovery Laboratory, University of Massachusetts Amherst

**Jeff Jonas**, Chief Scientist and Founder, Systems Research & Development

**Dr. Takeo Kanade**, U.A. Helen Whitaker University Professor of Computer Science and Robotics, Carnegie Mellon University

**Nuala O'Connor Kelly**, Chief Privacy Officer, Department of Homeland Security

**Dr. Thomas H. Killion**, Acting Deputy Assistant Secretary for Research and Technology/Chief Scientist, Department of Defense

**George B. Lotz, II**, Assistant to the Secretary of Defense (Intelligence Oversight)

**Teresa Lunt**, Principal Scientist and Area Manager of Security Group and Area Manager of Theory Group, Palo Alto Research Center

**The Hon. Paul McHale**, Assistant Secretary of Defense for Homeland Defense

**Judith A. Miller**, Williams & Connolly

**Lieutenant Colonel Ronald K. Miller**, United States Air Force

**Vahan Moushegian**, Director, Privacy Office, Department of Defense

**The Hon. Representative Jerry Nadler** (D-N.Y.)

**Major General Paul D. Nielsen**, Commander, Air Force Research Laboratory, Wright-Patterson Air Force Base, Ohio

**Sue Payton**, Deputy Under Secretary of Defense (Advanced Systems & Concepts)

**Dr. Gregory Piatetsky-Shapiro**, President, KDnuggets

**Dr. Robert Popp**, Special Assistant to the Director for Strategic Matters, DARPA

**Vito Potenza**, Acting General Counsel, National Security Agency

**Michael R. Ramage**, General Counsel, Florida Department of Law Enforcement

**Thomas M. Regan**, Executive Director for Privacy and Regulatory Affairs, LexisNexis

**Martha Rogers**, Partner, Peppers & Rogers

**Paul Rosenzweig**, Senior Legal Research Fellow, Heritage Foundation

**Dr. Nils R. Sandell, Jr.**, President and CEO, ALPHATEH, Inc.

**Brian Sharkey**, Senior Vice President, Advanced Systems and Concepts, Hicks & Associates

**Jeffrey H. Smith**, Arnold & Porter

**Jim Smyser**, Associate Deputy General Counsel (Military Personnel and Reserve Policy)

**David Sobel**, General Counsel, Electronic Privacy and Information Center

**Jay Stanley**, Communications Director, American Civil Liberties Union

**James B. Steinberg**, Vice President and Director, Foreign Policy Studies, Brookings Institution

**Dr. Latanya Sweeney**, Director, Laboratory for International Data Privacy, Carnegie Mellon University

**Captain David C. Taylor**, United States Navy, Chief, J6 Director's Action Group

**Dr. Anthony J. Tether**, Director, Defense Advanced Research Projects Agency

**Stephen Thayer**, Deputy Director, Office of National Risk Assessment, Department of Homeland Security

**Michael Vatis**, Executive Director, Markle Foundation Task Force on National Security in the Information Age

**Allan Wade**, Chief Information Officer, Central Intelligence Agency

**The Hon. Senator Ron Wyden** (D-Ore.)

**The Hon. Michael W. Wynne**, Acting Under Secretary of Defense (Acquisition, Technology and Logistics)

**Lee M. Zeichner**, President, Zeichner Risk Analytics, LLC

Mr. CANNON. Ms. O'Connor Kelly.

## TESTIMONY OF NUALA O'CONNOR KELLY, CHIEF PRIVACY OFFICER, U.S. DEPARTMENT OF HOMELAND SECURITY

Ms. O'CONNOR KELLY. Chairman Cannon, Ranking Member Watt, Chairman Chabot, Ranking Member Nadler, Members of Subcommittees and distinguished colleagues on the panel, it is my great honor to be before you on behalf of the United States Department of Homeland Security's Privacy Office, which I am privileged to lead as the Department's first Chief Privacy Officer.

I am pleased to offer my reflections on the findings and recommendations of the 9/11 Commission Report and also on the Report of the Department of Defense, TAPAC, particularly as they relate to the privacy of individuals.

As the first statutorily-mandated Privacy Officer in the Federal Government in a role that provides both investigative oversight and policy advice, I am keenly aware of the challenges presented by the Commission's role. In every respect, the 9/11 Commission has met those daunting challenges admirably, and I know I join every American in thanking them for their work.

The Report teaches us that one of the reasons the United States failed to prevent the September 11 attacks was its failure to think creatively.

As the Commission's work points out, our future requires new and creative modes of thinking and demands that we institutionalize new and imaginative mindsets within the very culture and structure of our Federal Government. Most importantly, we must perform our tasks in a manner that respects the privacy, the dignity and the personal freedoms of each individual in the United States.

Just as the Commission recommends institutionalizing imagination, we at the Department of Homeland Security have already begun operationalizing privacy awareness within the very culture of our organization. This has meant both responding to privacy complaints from within and outside the Department and actively raising privacy awareness across each of our directorates.

We have crafted privacy training and privacy policies for many of our new programs, ensured that the statutorily-required privacy impact assessments and system of record notices are written and reviewed, and counseled DHS officials regarding the effective and responsible uses of new technologies.

Outside of our organization, we have reached to advocacy groups, to our partners in the European Union and throughout the world and to the general public for input and guidance on our programs. We are vigorously pursuing our statutory mission of ensuring that the Department's technologies and programs sustain, and do not erode, privacy protections relating to the collection, use and disclosure of personal information.

No one has been a greater champion in these efforts than Secretary Tom Ridge, who from the very inception of our Department has recognized that privacy is a vital thread that runs through the fabric of the United States. Privacy is a value today that we seek to protect, as we protect both the tangible and intangible assets of our country through all of our endeavors at the Department.

I wish to thank Secretary Ridge and also Deputy Secretary Loy and commend them for their leadership and active support of my role and for the efforts of the DHS Privacy Office, including our more than 430 Privacy and Freedom of Information Act specialists throughout the Department.

The wisdom that Congress demonstrated when it mandated a Chief Privacy Officer and an integrated Privacy Office within the Department of Homeland Security represents precisely the kind of bold and creative thinking that will be demanded of our leaders and policymakers in the post-9/11 world. As the United States transforms its Federal intelligence and law enforcement communities, operationalizing privacy protections across the Federal Government, it is imperative that we sustain this dialogue among policymakers, technologists, intelligence professionals, law enforcement officials and also the private sector.

The Commission's recommendations raise a number of points that are crucial to bear in mind as we move ahead in this new process. The Commission points out that the choice between security and liberty is a false choice. We as a Nation must abandon the pessimistic and misguided notion that in order to be safe we must sacrifice the privacy of our personal information. The Department of Homeland Security's Privacy Office has worked tirelessly to demonstrate that the dichotomy between liberty and security is a false one by working in partnership with program and policy personnel to embed privacy within successful security initiatives from the very beginning.

As we seek to combine information in new and creative ways in the Federal Government, we must also establish and enforce concrete safeguards that prevent the Federal Government from exceeding its boundaries. As the Commission correctly points out, the burden should be on policymakers to prove that any new power granted to the Government is accompanied by adequate guidelines and oversight to properly confine its use.

The Commission's report findings heavily underscore the need to abandon the compartmentalized structure of our intelligence bureaucracy that existed before 9/11 and move to a more integrated system. Congress should permit agencies to share and disclose information collected for counterterrorism purposes if such sharing and disclosure is necessary and appropriate to achieve a security function. However, agencies should also demonstrate an adherence to privacy principles and fair information practices, including educating employees about the purposeful and responsible use of information.

A final matter is the recommendation of the Commission that the President appoint a board within the executive branch to oversee adherence to these guidelines and recommend the commitment the Government makes to defend its civil liberties.

We are keenly aware in our office of the benefit of having a central, coordinating privacy authority that is both knowledgeable about organizational structures and yet independent enough to act as an effective privacy advocate. It is one of the greatest challenges and opportunities of our office that we serve both outside and inside roles in the structure of our agency. The Chief Privacy Officer is appointed by the Secretary, but also is a position created by Congress and reports to Congress. The dual aspects of this role have allowed our office to turn a critical eye on the most controversial and also mundane aspects of the Department's operations, while offering a supporting hand to our key decisionmakers.

Any privacy oversight body in a sense must also be both outside and inside the Federal Government. Any such body must combine real knowledge of ongoing activities with real authority to confront and prevent abuse. I look forward to sharing my own experiences and participating in the public dialogue on such a matter in the coming months.

I extend my deepest gratitude to Chairman Cannon and to the Members of the Subcommittee for your oversight and interest in our office, and I thank you for your time and attention.

Mr. CANNON. Thank you, and thank you to all the Members of the panel.

[The prepared statement of Ms. O'Connor Kelly follows:]

PREPARED STATEMENT OF NUALA O'CONNOR KELLY

Chairman Cannon, Ranking Member Watt, Members of the Subcommittee, and distinguished colleagues on this panel, it is an honor to testify before you today regarding the 9/11 Commission on behalf of the United States Department of Homeland Security's Privacy Office, which I am privileged to lead as the first Chief Privacy Officer.

I am pleased to offer my reflections on the findings and recommendations of the 9/11 Commission's report. That Commission was charged by Congress and our President with the important yet daunting task of investigating this tragic event in our history with an eye toward implementing future changes. As the first statutorily-mandated Privacy Officer in the Federal Government, and as someone who provides both investigative oversight and policy advice, I am keenly aware of the challenges presented by the Commission's role. It is a role that requires both tenacity and discretion, persistent determination and unyielding patience, meticulous attention to detail and perceptive understanding of the "bigger picture". In every respect, the 9/11 Commission has met those daunting challenges admirably, and I know that I join every American when I commend and thank them for their fine work.

We have heard from the Commission's Report that among the many reasons for the United States government's failure to prevent those dreadful attacks was a failure to think creatively about the challenges we faced and to act upon information we received. In the words of the Commission, we suffered a "failure of imagination". Looking forward, it is clear from the Commission's work that the years ahead will require new and creative modes of thinking and will demand that we "institutionalize" new, imaginative mindsets within the very culture and structures of our government. Most importantly, we must perform these tasks in a manner that respects the privacy, dignity, and personal freedoms of every individual who lives in and visits the United States. Indeed, years from now, we will be said to have suffered yet another tragic "failure of imagination" if, while undertaking efforts to reform our intelligence community and protect our security, we fail to think and act creatively to protect privacy as well.

ONE YEAR ONWARD: PROTECTING PRIVACY WITHIN DHS

My firm belief, which has been affirmed by my experiences during the past year, is that protecting both privacy and security is well within the grasp of our collective imagination. In fact, during my first year as the Chief Privacy Officer of our Department, I have operated under that very premise, and have worked to ensure that privacy and security go hand-in-hand as we carry out our protective mission. In much the same way that the 9/11 Commission recommends "institutionalizing imagination", we at the Department of Homeland Security have begun instituting and operationalizing privacy awareness within the very culture of our organization. We have done so by working side-by-side with senior leadership and by ensuring that as programs move forward to implementation, they have been carefully and thoroughly analyzed for their impact on personal privacy. This has meant responding to privacy complaints from inside and outside the Department and actively raising awareness of privacy across all of our directorates. We have crafted privacy training and privacy policies for many of our programs, ensured that statutorily-required Privacy Impact Assessments and System of Records Notices are written and reviewed, and counseled DHS officials regarding the effective and responsible use of technology. Beyond our organization, we have reached out to advocacy groups and the general public for input and guidance. Moreover, on the international level, we have reached important agreements with our partners in the EU and elsewhere, and have participated in fruitful discussions with organizations like the International Association of Data Protection and Privacy Commissioners. In short, my office is vigorously pursuing its statutory missions, including ensuring that DHS technologies "sustain, and do not erode, privacy protections relating to the use, collection, and disclosure of personal information."

It is not an accident that DHS in its very first year began linking the values of homeland security and privacy protection as being compatible rather than opposing goals. It was a well thought out legislative design, firmly embedded in Section 222 of the Homeland Security Act, to reflect fundamental American values. No one has been a greater champion of this pairing of values than Secretary Tom Ridge, who from the very beginning has set the direction "from the top" that privacy, matters of individual dignity, and civil liberties define the fabric of America that we seek to protect in all of our endeavors at DHS. Today, I wish to thank Secretary Ridge publicly and commend him for his leadership and active support for the role and efforts of the Privacy Office at DHS and the entire Privacy team, which includes more than 430 Privacy Act and Freedom of Information specialists who work throughout the Department.

## LOOKING FORWARD: PRIVACY ACROSS THE FEDERAL GOVERNMENT

The wisdom Congress demonstrated when it mandated a Privacy Officer within DHS represents precisely the kind of bold and creative thinking that will be demanded of our leaders and policy-makers in a post 9/11 world. As the United States transforms its federal intelligence and law enforcement communities, operationalizing privacy protections across all of government will be more imperative, and more challenging, than ever. It will require, first and foremost, sustained dialogue among policy makers, technologists, intelligence professionals, law enforcement officials, and the private sector. The Commission's Report has provided an excellent starting point for that dialogue. Their recommendations raise a number of points that are crucial to bear in mind as we move ahead in this process.

First, as the Commission quite correctly points out, "the choice between security and liberty is a false choice". We as a nation must abandon, once and for all, the notion that in order to be safe, we must give up our right to keep our personal information private. As the recent TAPAC Report concluded, "The stakes on both sides—guarding against attacks and protecting privacy—could not be higher. We must not sacrifice one for the other. . . ." Within DHS, the Privacy Office has worked tirelessly to prove this point, and to demonstrate that the sometimes perceived dichotomy between liberty and security is a false one. As I have said on numerous occasions, the protection of privacy is neither an adjunct, nor the antithesis to, the mission of the Department of Homeland Security. Rather, privacy protection is, in fact, at the core of that mission. Likewise, privacy protection must also be at the core of our national mission as we devise ways to reform and improve our intelligence and anti-terrorist efforts.

One way that we as a nation can put to rest the perceived dichotomy between liberty and security is by unleashing the vast potential of our technology. Too often, advances in technology are met with concern and trepidation. Yet, just as our technology can be misused to suppress privacy, so too can it be used to enhance and protect it. During my time as Chief Privacy Officer, I have observed first-hand how technology solutions can greatly enhance the privacy of individuals. Technical features such as encryption, audit trails, one-way hash functions, and tiered access control modules, among others, make it possible to analyze information in a way that protects people's safety while limiting access to personal information and preserving the integrity of data. Moreover, as technologists know quite well, information security is paramount to protecting privacy. Therefore, the key to ensuring that technologies used by our government sustain and do not erode privacy will be to harness the creative energy of those who design and implement our technical infrastructures, challenging them to devise new solutions that secure and protect our personal information.

## OVERSIGHT AND GUIDELINES

Technology and privacy awareness, while important, will not be enough to address our current challenges. As we move forward, we will also need to establish and enforce concrete safeguards that prevent government from exceeding its proper bounds. As the Commission correctly points out, the burden should be on policymakers to prove that any new power granted to government is accompanied by "adequate guidelines and oversight to properly confine its use." The idea here is an important one—privacy protections must be put in place at the front-end of our governmental processes when programs are in their infancy, rather than later, after privacy abuses and mistakes have already taken place.

The United States has a firm foundation upon which to build additional privacy protections. Existing laws such as the Privacy Act of 1974, the Freedom of Information Act, and the E-Government Act all seek to embed "fair information practices" and a general respect for privacy into the daily operations of our government. Coupled with our Constitutional provisions, these statutes form an essential part of a privacy culture that will only become more relevant in the years to come. As we build upon this legacy of privacy protection, we must find ways to embed these values within the new statutory frameworks that will govern the collection, use, sharing, and retention of intelligence and other personal information.

Much of the 9/11 Commission Report's comments in this area address the need to integrate and coordinate the data that are collected for our antiterrorism efforts more effectively. The Report's findings underscore the need to abandon the compartmentalized structure of our intelligence bureaucracy that existed before 9/11 and move to a more integrated system. It is my view that Congress should permit agencies to establish clear parameters for sharing information to protect privacy. As some have said, we must move from a "need to know" to a "need to share". Establishing reasonable limits on access and embedding fair use principles will be important, not only because it will protect individuals, but also because it will engender the kind of trust in government that is necessary to achieve the cooperation of both the public and private sectors. In failing to abide by these principles, we risk replacing the problem of "stove-pipes", in which disparate pieces of information are never adequately integrated, with one of "leaky pipes", in which personal information is exposed for all to see.

## CREATING AN OVERSIGHT BODY FOR PRIVACY AND CIVIL LIBERTIES

I would like to address, as a final matter, the recommendation of the Commission that the President appoint "a board within the executive branch to oversee adherence to the guidelines we recommend and the commitment the government makes to defend our civil liberties."

I am keenly aware of the benefits of having a central, coordinating privacy authority that is both knowledgeable enough about organizational structures to obtain information and yet independent enough to act as an effective privacy advocate. It has been one of the greatest advantages of my position at DHS that I serve concomitant roles both inside and outside the structures of our agency. The Chief Privacy officer is appointed by the Secretary, but is a position created by statute and required to report to Congress. The dual aspects of this role have allowed me to turn a critical eye on the most controversial and the most ordinary aspects of the Department's operations, while also offering a supportive hand to key decision-makers. I do not see my office as the enemy of the missions of the Department. Rather, I see it as crucial to achieving that mission successfully.

Implementing such an oversight position for the entire federal government is admittedly a different task, one that would require attention to matters of a completely different nature and scale. Since the government's response to the 9/11 Commission's recommendations is still being formulated, it is too early to say precisely what type of body will best address the privacy needs of our Federal Government. While the challenges and responsibilities faced by the person or persons who undertake this responsibility will be distinct from those faced by the Chief Privacy Officer at DHS, I look forward to sharing my own experiences and participating in the public dialogue on this matter in the coming months.

## CONCLUSION

Each and every one of the issues raised by the 9/11 Commission regarding the upholding of personal privacy presents a unique but highly important challenge to our nation. Facing these challenges will require extraordinary imagination. The exercise of that imagination and the implementation of the resulting changes certainly will not be easy. And yet as Thomas Jefferson wisely noted, "It is part of the American character to consider nothing as desperate; to surmount every difficulty with resolution. . . ." If there is any over-arching lesson to be learned from the fine work of the 9/11 Commission, it is precisely that. Three years after the 9/11 attacks on New York and Washington, and in the memory of those who passed in the fields of Pennsylvania, our nation is united in its desire to learn from the past by re-organizing and reforming antiterrorism efforts. At the same time, we seek to renew our foundational commitment to respecting the privacy of each individual, as a matter of law and policy. As the DHS Privacy Officer, I work daily to ensure that this sacred commitment—our unwavering determination to secure both our liberty *and* our land—is a guiding force behind every decision at the Department of Homeland Security. Thanks to the fine work of this Subcommittee, I am quite confident that our commitment to the protection of individual privacy will continue to guide anti-terrorism efforts not only within DHS, but across our entire Federal Government.

I would like to extend my deepest gratitude to you, Chairman Cannon and to the Members of the Subcommittee for your tireless work and enduring contribution to our nation. Thank you today for your time and attention. I would be happy to respond to your questions.

Mr. CANNON. I think we are going to proceed by seniority on each side of the dais, beginning with the co-Chairman of this panel, Mr. Chabot.

Mr. CHABOT. I did mention in my opening statement that I have a particular interest in H.R. 338, the Federal Agency Protection of Privacy Act, formerly known as the Defense of Privacy Act, it is basically the same bill, and I think, Senator Gorton and Secretary Marsh, you have both mentioned that in your testimony.

A number of us were very concerned and have been for years that too often when regulations or rules were promulgated by various agencies that privacy protections of the American people too often were kind of an afterthought and were not necessarily taken into consideration, and they should be up front.

In essence, what this Act requires is—we all know about environmental impact statements—is basically a privacy impact statement. What it amounts to is to determine whether or not the agency has taken into consideration privacy issues and maybe there was an alternative way to be less intrusive on those privacy rights, just to make sure we are looking at these things ahead of time.

I actually introduced this back in the 106th Congress; and our colleague, Congressman Bob Barr, took it up in the 107th. We reintroduced it; and I want to thank my Ranking Member, Mr. Nadler from New York, for cosponsoring this and also Chairman Cannon for cosponsoring this as well. But it passed in the Judiciary Committee back on July 7, so it will be moving hopefully to the floor in the near future.

But I would be interested to hear from the panel members as to how they think—and I know, Senator, I think you stated you cannot necessarily recommend for or against legislation, but how do you think this could potentially impact the issues that we are talking about here relative to the 9/11 Commission?

Mr. GORTON. We in the 9/11 Commission took sort of a self-denying ordinance, you know, in not going beyond the recommendations that we made. We were perhaps as surprised as we were delighted that we were able to come out unanimously, and that required a degree of self-restraint. So we cannot take a particular position on your bill. But we can say it is quite consistent. It certainly seems to proceed from the same philosophy that guided us in asking for the creation of this board to see to the protection of the civil liberties from any new powers granted in the war against terrorism.

Mr. CHABOT. Thank you.

Secretary Marsh, I didn't know if you wanted to add anything.

Mr. MARSH. I believe that it would be helpful to give it more of a defense or national security flavor for those portions that involve the Department of Defense or the Intelligence Community, and they have to be singled out because they are going to have to be treated differently. But I think it is a step in the right direction.

If you look at the recommendations of the Committee Report, they are very elaborate recommendations on establishing a regime or protocol of how to do this, and it involves the President of the United States. We are suggesting also overview, not because they are not going to do a good job but simply to emphasize the importance of what is being done by the legislation.

I think the legislation is a very good starting point, Congressman; and I welcome it. It is responsive to one of our problems.

Mr. CHABOT. Thank you very much.

I am probably not going to be able to get into a lot, I have 1 minute left, but one of the other areas that I wanted to delve into, maybe some of my colleagues will, is one of the recommendations of the 9/11 Commission Report that stated, "At this time of increased and consolidated Government authority, there should be a board within the executive branch to oversee adherence to the guidelines we recommend and the commitment the Government makes to defend our civil liberties."

I think prior to deciding the structure of an organization there must be a clear understanding of that organization's mission. So there are a number of questions that I think at some point it would be very helpful to get into, such as does the 9/11 Commission view the board recommended in the report as being limited to examining privacy, or should it weigh in on all things related to the nexus between civil liberties and Government action, and would the board be charged with evaluating security against privacy protections and would it be a watchdog or a facilitator.

There are many aspects that I think we would be interested to get into, but my time has already wound up here, so I will yield back my time at this point.

Mr. CANNON. The gentleman yields back.

Mr. Nadler, would you like to take the next 5 minutes?

Mr. NADLER. Thank you, Mr. Chairman.

Congressman Hamilton, Senator Gorton, in your statement, in your joint statement, you said that the test, referring to the PATRIOT Act and some other things, the test is a simple but important one. The burden of proof should be on the proponents of the measure to establish that the power or authority being sought would in fact materially enhance national security and that there will be adequate supervision of the exercise of that power or authority to ensure protection of civil liberties. It is sort of a but-for test: but for this power, would we be less safe?

This Committee has repeatedly asked the Attorney General that question with respect—or at least some Members of this Committee have repeatedly asked the Attorney General that question with respect to various provisions of the PATRIOT Act, and we have been unable to get any specific responses.

In other words, if this power which the PATRIOT Act grants had existed pre-9/11, would—if that power had existed pre-9/11, would it have made a difference in preventing 9/11, for example, in your opinion? We have been unable to get any answers on that.

So my question is, in light of that experience, with respect to the privacy board or privacy officers you are proposing, what steps do you think that we need to take to ensure that these officials, one, are independent; two, are able to get the information that they need to get in order to do their work—information, as I said, this Committee can often not get; and, three, that they have the clout needed to have an impact?

Mr. HAMILTON. Well, Mr. Nadler, those are difficult questions to answer because they really go to the power of the Congress to conduct effective oversight. And my view, I guess not the Commission's view—I shouldn't try to speak for the Commission at this point—but I am very concerned about the lack of robustness, if you would, or aggressiveness, in congressional oversight today.

We did not try to get into the specifics of the PATRIOT Act, except with regard to the one provision on the wall of separation, but we did suggest this test for any official, and that is as deeply as we went into it.

When the executive does not respond to the Congress—and, incidentally, we hear that complaint often in our appearing before different Committees. It appears to me that the problem is quite pervasive in the executive-congressional relationship. It is not anything that is new. It goes back for a good many years.

I think there is a lot of timidity in the Congress with regard to its exercise of oversight and, at the end of the day, they are only going to pay attention to you if you have budget authority with them.

Mr. NADLER. That brings up the real question I am asking, which is not simply—I think that this Congress has been very timid in exercising oversight, too, but that is really a separate issue.

My point was that we have been unable to get the information, and in light of that experience, if we are to establish this privacy board, these privacy officers that you are recommending, what do we have to do to make sure that they can get the information that we have not been able to get, that they can get information that they need once we have established that they are independent and that they have the clout? What powers do we have to give them, what authority do we have to give them to make sure they can do the job that you are outlining for us?

Mr. HAMILTON. Mr. Nadler, we simply did not try to get into the details of the powers that the board would have.

You mentioned I think a moment ago that Congress has to fill in the details, and this is a major detail that you would have to fill in. My own personal view is the board should have quite robust powers. But the important thing here to recognize is that what we have recommended calls for a great deal of Government intervention and strengthening of Government powers over individual lives. That is just inherent in counterterrorism policy. You are greatly expanding the role of Government when you are fighting terrorists, and we think it is necessary because of the threat.

Mr. NADLER. Could I have 1 additional minute?

Mr. CANNON. Without objection.

Mr. HAMILTON. You have to have some check on that expansion.

Mr. NADLER. Which brings me to the other question I wanted to ask, and that is an internal board cannot take the place, in my opinion, of meaningful court oversight, so to what extent do you think—so Secretary Marsh is probably the better person to ask this question to—to what extent should there be court judicial review of the actions or lack of actions of this board or these privacy officers?

Mr. MARSH. Well, we recommend that there be oversight internally and that the oversight will be in the courts. We feel that court review at various junctures of this is a very, very powerful method of protecting——

Mr. NADLER. So it shouldn't be an arbitrary and capricious standard. You should have better access?

Mr. MARSH. We insist on access to the FISA courts wherever you are dealing with a U.S. person.

Mr. CANNON. The gentleman's time has expired.

Mr. NADLER. Thank you, Mr. Chairman.

Mr. CANNON. Do you want another minute or two?

Mr. NADLER. I would.

Mr. CANNON. Without objection, the gentleman is recommended for an additional 2 minutes.

Mr. NADLER. Senator Gorton seems to be interested in answering this, too. The question I would like you to address is, the courts should have oversight, but very often, in fact, even usually, the courts' oversight of administrative agencies is limited to an arbitrary and capricious standard, which means that what the agency does generally goes, unless their conduct is really egregious. Should we establish some other standard for reviews and give the courts more power, in effect, to second-guess what this board or these privacy officers might do or not do?

Mr. GORTON. Mr. Nadler, I have three points in answer to your very good question.

First, in the two areas, really both relating to the wall and on which we did express an opinion, that portion of the PATRIOT Act met the tests that we had set out. That was number one.

Number two, you all, in your wisdom, of course, passed the PATRIOT Act with an expiration date.

Mr. NADLER. Part of it has an expiration date.

Mr. GORTON. At least as far as that part is concerned, you have the ultimate power. The Justice Department, obviously, is going to have to answer your questions, or you are going to have to lie down and ignore a failure to do so. But that is probably the greatest single power that you reserved to yourself, to see to it that you as the Congress get——

Mr. NADLER. But the privacy officers and this board are not going to have to the power to do this. What do we give them?

Mr. GORTON. We recommended the creation of a board that could protect these rights. As Lee said, we have not gone into all of the details as to where it should be. Some the Members thought it ought to be in the Department of Justice. I think, given your questions, you are probably inclined to believe that it ought to be an independent agency or board.

Those are decisions for you all to make, as are the decisions as to the degree of the review for it or the right of an individual to sue outside of the system with respect to the law.

Mr. NADLER. I am less concerned where we put it than what powers they have, how independent it is, and how we can enforce the executive branch to comply with the decisions it makes.

Mr. GORTON. It should be independent, and it should be powerful enough so that it gets listened to.

Mr. NADLER. Thank you. Thank you, Mr. Chairman.

Mr. CANNON. The gentleman yields back.

I hope the panel and also the Members of the two Committees will consider that, in dealing with these details, we may not have enough information. We may need to be considering a commission that will help us think through some of the details, because I share the concerns of the gentleman from New York on how we go about this.

The gentleman from Arizona, Mr. Flake, is recognized for 5 minutes.

Mr. FLAKE. I thank the Chairmen, both Mr. Chabot and Mr. Cannon, for organizing this hearing and the witnesses for coming.

I want to thank the 9/11 Commission for its particular focus on secure sources of identification. That has been something that I have been concerned about for a couple of years. I introduced legislation last year, H.R. 3461, to require States, if they want their State driver's license used as a form of Federal identification, or identification for Federal purposes, that there have to be some kind of standards there. Because, as it stands, if a State like California doesn't use the same kind of standards or uses lax standards, it doesn't affect just the citizens of California, it affects all of us, because it is used increasingly as the closest form of a national ID as we have. When it is used for air travel and other things, there is certainly a Federal nexus there.

We also have created more of a Federal nexus when we allow, with the Help America Vote Act, an individual State to allow them to use a driver's license as a form of identification to register to vote. So there is a Federal nexus here, and I am pleased with the Commission's focus on this.

I would just like to get your thoughts on it and how quickly we ought to move to that. My bill specifically says if a State wants its drivers' licenses used as a form of Federal ID, it has to have some kind of standard.

You have also talked about standards for birth certificates, because those are the sort of breeder documents that are then used to secure these forms of ID. Can you give some elaboration on those things? Mr. Hamilton?

Mr. HAMILTON. Mr. Flake, thank you for the question.

I think we do suggest in our recommendations that there be Federal standards applied to these identification documents, birth certificates, driver's licenses and a lot of other things. That has to be seen in a broader context, and the context is that we need, we believe, a modern border immigration system. You have to look at all the ways that people get into the United States, and you need to stress biometric exit and entry systems. You have got to give these officials that check people coming into the country, whether it is by land, sea or air, access to information with regard to visitors and immigrants.

You have to have in your Intelligence Community the ability to look at the indicators of terrorist travel. Terrorists have to travel a lot. You have to develop an exchange of information with other countries so that you can make, for example, a real-time verification of passports, and you are going to have to involve a lot more local and State officials.

Now, all of those things go together with what you are talking about; and the secure identification of U.S. citizens becomes very, very important in letting the right people in and keeping the bad people out.

Mr. FLAKE. What I found was quite striking as well. In Arizona, my 16-year-old son just went and got his driver's license. His driver's license is good, I think, until he is age 65. He can get a driver's license theoretically, and he did, for 44 years.

Now, somebody entering the country, for other States to do this—gratefully, Arizona does this right. It doesn't anymore offer a driver's license for a period longer than the expiration of a visa. But only 11 States operate that way.

In other States that offer—and I don't know how many will allow you to get a 44-year license, but if you come on a student visa for 6 months or a year or 2 years, you can get a license for up to 20 or 30 or perhaps even 44 years, and there is your de facto ID. And we know that two of the terrorists on 9/11 had overstayed, yet they had licenses from States that existed for longer than their visa.

Senator Gorton, do you feel that is an important part as well, to ensure that a driver's license, because it is used as a form of Federal ID, if you will, not be issued for a longer period than the stay of the visa?

Mr. GORTON. Well, again, the Commission didn't judge that specific idea. We did speak, as Lee has said, to birth certificates and driver's licenses, because driver's licenses are the most common form of identification and our concentration was on having uniform standards for them. You are talking about a form of uniform standards, at least.

We are concerned not so much about their length, though that is an important consideration, as their validity, as really identifying who a person is. That is where our concentration lies.

Mr. FLAKE. Thank you.

Thank you, Mr. Chairman.

Mr. CANNON. The gentleman yields back.

I am quite certain the gentleman from Iowa, when he has the opportunity to speak, is going to be concerned about that issue, as I think many of the members of this panel are.

Mr. Scott, would you like to take 5 minutes?

Before you do so, let me just point out that the Ranking Member has graciously agreed to defer in the event that others have to leave. So we have not skipped over Mr. Watt, but he has been gracious in letting others go first.

Mr. Scott.

Mr. SCOTT. Thank you, Mr. Chairman.

Mr. Hamilton, with the extra powers for information gathering, wiretapping, data mining and whatnot, did the Commission limit these extra powers to terrorism-related investigations? The PATRIOT Act was not limited to terrorism, and some of us had some concerns about that. Had it been confined to terrorism, it might not have been as controversial. These extra powers may be extended to any kind of criminal investigation.

Mr. HAMILTON. Well, Mr. Scott, our focus was on terrorism, and when we recommended, as we do in several places, an expansion of Government power, we were limiting it to terrorism.

Mr. SCOTT. Do I understand that you did not recommend a national ID card?

Mr. HAMILTON. We did not.

Mr. SCOTT. The no-fly lists have obviously been over-inclusive from time to time, as the recent situation with Senator Kennedy is just one of the most recent examples. How many false positives should we be tolerating before we—I guess the more people you stop and keep off the plane, the more likely it is that one of them might actually be a terrorist. What kind of tolerance should we have for these false positives?

Mr. GORTON. Well, you know, our goal should be no false positives. But one of the reasons that we were so interested in this subject is that on 9/11 the FAA's no-fly list had 16 or 18 names on it. That is all. Part of our reason for a National Intelligence Director and a National Counterterrorism Center, was at the same time the State Department had a list of several thousand people that it suspected to be terrorists and the FAA didn't even know that the list existed. They learned about it at one of our hearings earlier this year.

So we do think that there should be an integration of valid terrorist information about the methods that these terrorists used to attack the United States. But it is obviously wrong to, you know, confuse one name for another. Just because there is one bad guy named Edward Kennedy doesn't mean Senator Kennedy should be kept off. We have got to be very careful, it seems to me, to see to it that the lists are real lists that identify real people and don't have a significant number of false positives.

Mr. SCOTT. Thank you.

Secretary Marsh, a lot of the data mining information went to the level of personalization of the lists and the information but didn't really go to the kind of information that we are talking about. What kind of information can be obtained in this data mining? Are we talking about, I guess, library records, travel records, credit, medical? Exactly what are we talking about?

Mr. MARSH. The databases actually can cover a very broad range of different subjects. They could cover travel, they could cover finance, they can cover possibly health records, if you get an exception.

The data mining is an accepted and very effective process. It is not new. We did data mining with fingerprints and law records years ago, but it is now so sophisticated because of computerization and it can reach so far and it reaches across boundaries and it can be international.

What we need are methodologies, and I think a number are being developed, whereby we can confine those lists very quickly and minimize what we have to have, and then anonymize, so there is no disclosure of who you are looking at until you reach the point.

Mr. SCOTT. One of the things we had—I am not sure what the status of it is now—the FBI guidelines used to be that you wouldn't gather information unless you were actually investigating a specific crime or had some specific investigation. You just wouldn't gather information.

Mr. MARSH. I believe that was in law enforcement, wasn't it?

Mr. SCOTT. Well, are we mining this data just for generalized——

Mr. MARSH. That which is done—defense criteria on data mining is different than law enforcement. But in defense that is done toward a specific objective, and inside the NSA you will find that they are very specifically oriented. I think there are 650 million intercepts a day that are filtered through. But they are very specific; and they are looking at a suspicious, threatening person and using a general pattern search to try and find that person.

Mr. CANNON. Does the gentleman desire additional time?

Mr. SCOTT. Could I follow through on that, Mr. Chairman?

Mr. CANNON. Without objection, the gentleman is recognized for an additional 2 minutes.

Mr. SCOTT. Thank you.

Well, are we looking after a specific person to track him down in terms of travel and who he is contacting? Still, you are looking at one specific person, not just going into a database and seeing what pops out.

Mr. MARSH. Right. Correct.

Mr. SCOTT. So you mentioned in law enforcement we are relegated to waiting until you are actually investigating a crime. In this case, are you just gathering information?

Mr. MARSH. For intelligence purposes, yes.

Mr. SCOTT. Is this United States citizens?

Mr. MARSH. A United States citizen comes under a court order.

Mr. SCOTT. So you have to have particularized suspicion.

Mr. MARSH. That is right.

Mr. SCOTT. And probable cause.

Mr. MARSH. All the rules change when you have a U.S. person, which is a United States citizen, a permanent foreign resident or a U.S. Corporation that is not foreign controlled.

Mr. SCOTT. Thank you, Mr. Chairman.

Mr. CANNON. The gentleman yields back.

I guess we are at Mr. Forbes. Would you like to be recognized for 5 minutes?

Mr. FORBES. Thank you, Mr. Chairman.

Mr. Chairman, I would like to echo what you said earlier about the privilege that we have to be with such a distinguished panel and also to appreciate the comments of the Ranking Member today.

We have had a number of hearings in different Committees, and there have been some individuals who have run out to press conferences or made comments in the Committees about why we weren't just enacting all the recommendations without hearings. I think the comment that said that before we go anywhere we need to understand what the recommendations are and the ramifications of those recommendations is so true, and I thank you all for being here today and your patience in helping us do just that.

Let me go to my fellow Virginian for a question. Mr. Marsh, I would like to follow up on what Congressman Scott was saying. The first question I would have is so many people today are telling us that the only way we can have an adequate defense is to do some sort of risk assessment, some sort of risk assessment where we are concentrating our defenses, because we just have so many vulnerable areas, so it would be impossible to cover them all. Can we be effective in that risk assessment if we are not doing an effective job with data mining?

Mr. MARSH. The panel concluded that data mining is an absolutely essential tool for a counterterrorist program but that data mining program must be formalized, it must be established, it must be controlled, it must have procedures, it must be audited, and, if you are dealing with U.S. citizens, you must use the FISA court.

Mr. FORBES. Recently, we had a private citizen—that it was determined through the use of open-source information that a U.S. National Guardsman was plotting terrorist activities on his fellow soldiers. This was, obviously, a very ingenious way to find a terrorist before they could commit a terrorist act. Could you tell us if the TAPAC recommendations limit data mining for open source information?

Mr. MARSH. No. Not completely, no.

Mr. FORBES. They wouldn't.

One final thing. Do we have any idea what foreign countries are doing right now with data mining and how they are utilizing it? I am sure you studied that and analyzed that.

Mr. MARSH. There are significant private efforts offshore. Some of their programs are more strict and stern than ours. I believe the oldest is—I may be mistaken here, somebody help me—is Sweden.

What you have touched on, Mr. Congressman, a concern that exists in this community with this technology is that we have a lead, and we must maintain that lead, and there are abilities possibly by others to overtake us in that technological lead, and staying—staying in that lead is absolutely essential.

One of the recommendations of our panel is research on data mining that does not necessarily mean go do data mining but do the research to find what you can do, what are the capabilities you can achieve by doing it, simply in order to maintain a supremacy and lead, which we think in this struggle is absolutely essential.

Mr. FORBES. We found the same concern, as you know, with biological weapons. Because we had stopped a lot of our research on creating some of those weapons, so the counter to that was we also had stopped our research on the defense of those weapons. As you mentioned, this is a technological edge that we could lose in a matter of months if we are not careful in how we are handling that.

Mr. MARSH. It is my recollection that this very fine report talks in terms of addressing these research programs to achieve some of these ends, if I am not mistaken.

Mr. HAMILTON. Yes, we address that in very general terms.

Mr. FORBES. Mr. Chairman, thank you very much. Thank you.

Mr. CANNON. The gentleman yields back.

I think that Mr. King is next in line. The Vice Chairman of the Committee is going to be penultimate or next to penultimate. But, Mr. King, you are recognized for 5 minutes.

Mr. KING. Thank you, Mr. Chairman. Again, I thank you for holding these hearings today and also Chairman Chabot.

I appreciate the testimony of the panelists. I know you put a lot of hours and days into this endeavor and this interesting report that brings some solid recommendations out, and I have some questions about a number of those.

I reflect back, though, across some of the other questions and testimony, and Congressman Flake made mention of the Help America Vote Act. I would just point out there is not a requirement for a picture identification to be presented at this point. So there is an allowance there for a poll worker to request identification, but not a requirement. So when it comes to voting, we don't have any more credibility there than we have sometimes getting into the United States. Both of those things are important.

With the passport exception for the Western Hemisphere, one can come into the United States from any Nation in the Western Hemisphere, other than Cuba, alleging to be a United States citizen, simply by making, and I believe the language, statutory language, is a credible allegation of citizenship. If it were not for that, I might still be in Jamaica, by the way, and that is how I know that law. That might not be so bad. And I hear your recommendations on tightening that up.

With regard to Congressman Flake's questions, I would also add this point that I would associate myself with the remarks of Congressman Hamilton with regard to the security. I direct my first question to you, Congressman Hamilton—would you consider a biometric Social Security card to be a national ID card?

Mr. HAMILTON. I don't think we tried to make those kind of judgments. We on the Commission were no experts on this whole field—and it is a difficult one—of biometric measures, and we did not address that.

Mr. KING. Thank you. I wanted to make just a few remarks on the security of our borders and how we might tighten that up. But I really would focus my interests instead, because I think we have a gap in our focus here, on where these recommendations of the Commission might go. Some of the statements that were made and some of the language causes my curiosity to be piqued.

The failure to think creatively I recognize that, and I agree with that. But we have a Commission recommendation to bring this all under one leadership, one voice, and you looked at MI-5 and stepped away from that because it was a higher probability of violating privacy and individual liberty. So the soaring rhetoric of—let me see, what was that word I was looking for—the institutionalization of imagination, it captures my imagination.

I would like to be able to institutionalize imagination. I would like to be able to inspire that in all the people that can think outside the box and think creatively, and I would like to find a way to root out some of the linear thinkers within our intelligence departments and replace them with creative thinkers. And yet, if I were going to form an organization that would be shaping groupthink, I would want to have one person at the top, all information underneath there. I would want to have control of the budget and the hiring and firing process, and I would just about bet you if you put me at the top of that, I could create group-think within that organization. I might even do it without wanting to do so.

So my concern is that we end up creating an organization that does exactly what we are trying to avoid, and I direct my question or request for a response for that remark to Ms. O'Connor Kelly first.

Ms. O'CONNOR KELLY. Well, I would have to defer to the experts on the 9/11 Commission, as I am not the expert on the Intelligence Community.

Mr. KING. You are the institutionalization of imagination though, and I that is why I went to you.

Ms. O'CONNOR KELLY. Sure. Absolutely. And I think we were quoting language from the report. I think there are so many different ways we can create privacy oversight and privacy values in the Federal Government. We can look not only at our experience with the Department of Homeland Security and having a Privacy Office within the ministry or the Department, we can look internationally at the creation of privacy czars, privacy commissioners, data protection officials throughout the world, many of which sit as part of the Federal service but outside of any Federal agency. We can certainly look at our own history with privacy commissions in previous decades.

So I think that point is an excellent one. You can't legislate creativity. That is precisely a very good point. But you can create bodies that will be both self-analyzing and also create oversight structures within and outside the Federal Government that could hope to create the kind of value structure that you are all talking about today in protecting privacy and respecting individuality, while also achieving the security mission.

Mr. KING. Mr. Marsh, would you comment?

Mr. MARSH. Congressman, I think the real danger in your bill, in our recommendations, is that they will go through some sort of baptism of bureaucracy and they will become very, very bureaucratic, and instead of doing the innovative, creative things that they need to do. I think we need to avoid the creation of a bureaucracy there, and that is going to depend on the leadership. Because the nature of these types of programs are regulatory, and my experience has been with regulatory things you get into, actually, a very helpful and useful bureaucracy, but I am not sure that is the goal you are driving for here.

Mr. KING. Mr. Chairman, could I ask unanimous consent for an extra additional minute?

Mr. CANNON. Without objection, so ordered.

Mr. KING. Thank you, Mr. Chairman.

I would just direct my question to Senator Gorton then. Did you examine the successes, the historical successes of intelligence, as you put these recommendations together?

Mr. GORTON. The answer to that question is, yes, of course we have had successes in our intelligence during the course of a 45-year Cold War. But I think I would really like to answer your previous question, if I may.

We have had a decentralized system. We have had an FBI that didn't talk to the CIA, and a CIA that didn't talk to the Department of Defense intelligence agencies. Decentralization's ultimate reward was 9/11. What we are trying to do is to cure 9/11. And this is not to say that there wasn't imagination. I think there was a great deal of imagination on the part of the FBI agents in Arizona. I think there was imagination on the part of those who arrested Moussaoui. I think similar things have taken place in the CIA. But, in many cases, they didn't even get to the top of their own agencies, much less anyone in authority, say, in the White House, who could get the benefit of that imagination.

Our recommendations for a National Counterterrorism Center and for the National Intelligence Director are so that there is a focal point, someone who is entitled to get all of the information, say, on counterterrorism that comes up from each of these agencies, put that work together, task them to do things to fill in gaps or to fill in holes, and have it there before the National Security Council, before the policy centers so they can act on it.

If you read our report through, I think you will join me in saying we had a couple of presidents who had to be frustrated. They just weren't getting the information that they needed from this current stovepipe system where people were hugging onto bits of information they got, rather than using them and sharing them.

Mr. KING. Did any agency get it right?

Mr. CANNON. Would the gentleman like an additional 2 minutes?

Mr. KING. One would be plenty, Mr. Chairman.

Mr. CANNON. Without objection, so ordered.

Mr. KING. Did any agency get it right?

Mr. GORTON. Well, if you say did any agency get it right in a way that prevented 9/11, of course, the answer to that question is an obvious no.

Did the FBI get it right when it prosecuted those who perpetrated the first World Trade Center, yes, they did, treating it as a law enforcement matter. But then there was this wall. They couldn't talk to one another with their intelligence people, and that clearly contributed to 9/11.

Mr. KING. Thank you very much.

Mr. HAMILTON. Mr. King, some agencies got it more right than others. The CIA understood the threat of terrorism as well as anybody. They spoke about it; and in 1998 the Director of the CIA said, we have got a war going on here. The only problem is, nobody paid any attention to him. Nobody even within the CIA paid any attention to him, and the other intelligence agencies didn't pay any attention to him.

If you want a competition of ideas, which your question suggests, you have got to have a free flow of information, and that is what we didn't have. If you want group-think, it is the status quo that developed group-think. And what we are suggesting, I believe, is more vitality, more information in the system, which I think will bring about more competitive analysis.

Everybody wants more competitive analysis in theory; not everybody wants it in practice. But if you increase the flow of information from foreign intelligence and defense intelligence and homeland security intelligence and if you increase the flow of information from the CIA and the NSA and the NGA and the NRO and all of these other agencies that you have that now collect intelligence but keep it to themselves, or at least they did prior to 9/11, I think improvements have been made since 9/11, but what we are trying to do is, to pick up one your words, is to institutionalize all of this, to get more information flowing through the system.

We are certainly not trying to put all of the power in the National Intelligence Director so that that director controls what becomes the intelligence product.

Mr. KING. Thank you, Mr. Chairman.

Mr. MARSH. Mr. King, in reference to your earlier question——

Mr. CANNON. Mr. Marsh, we have had a note from the C-SPAN people. Many of you are not speaking closely enough into the mikes. I think, Mr. Hamilton, you have been doing that, so I didn't interrupt. If you would pull that mike closer to you.

That is much better.

Mr. MARSH. In order to make those sorts of regulatory efforts effective, you need to place a burden on the most senior officials of the Department—I am talking about the Secretary—and you need to establish a role for the President to have a responsibility, and then you need to have your senior people come in here and respond to your Committee as a form of oversight and as a form of legislative audit. Then I think you will see the system will function much better.

Mr. KING. Thank you.

Mr. CANNON. The gentleman yields back.

The gentleman from Florida, Mr. Feeney, is recognized for 5 minutes.

Mr. FEENEY. Thank you, Mr. Chairman, for these hearings.

Mr. Marsh, along those lines, I have read the TAPAC report. It is very well done. But the first seven of your 12 recommendations rely totally on the good will of the Secretary, and it is only the executive branch and congressional oversight that is addressed in your last five recommendations that will make sure future secretaries in not just this but other agencies will not just be dependent on goodwill. I would like to get back to that in a minute.

But the other report that is fascinating is the 9/11 Report, and I really commend the entire Commission represented here today by Senator Gorton and Congressman Hamilton. It is not just the detail and the breadth and the extraordinary way that you have addressed a host of wide-ranging issues, but it also I think puts you at a new standard of literary work for Government reports. It really is an animated way to deal with the technological and historical issues that led up to 9/11 and the terror we experienced on that day.

I have to tell you that I might be the only Member here that in the midst of a hurricane had a flashlight out because I couldn't put down the book. It is not Hemingway or Shakespeare, but I think Arthur Conan Doyle would be proud of what you have done.

Mr. HAMILTON. Put it right up there with Harry Potter.

Mr. FEENEY. Yes, and, unfortunately, I don't think you will receive any of the commissions for that.

But, having said that, Congressman Scott talked about some very interesting issues earlier, and he sort of drew the line between citizens and noncitizens and the right to access, to courts, et cetera. But it seems to me one of the things your report touches on is the huge difference in kind, not degree, but difference in kind between fighting crime and fighting actual intelligence threats.

What we do with respect to bank robbers is put 99 percent of our resources into capturing, prosecuting and then punishing the bank robber. That model doesn't work when the next plane could be full of biological, chemical or nuclear weapons. I think that is something Americans have to understand. We are dealing with a difference, not in degree, but of kind, in the way that we fight these things.

Much has been made of the stovepipes, and Congressman Hamilton just talked about the critical nature of the free flow of information internationally and then across Federal agency lines. I don't find much in your report on the recommendations, and I heard very little emphasis on the free flow of information to State and localities.

The last time the continental U.S. was attacked by a serious foreign threat was 1812 when the British burned down our Capitol. We now have for the first time since 1812 State law enforcement, we have got sheriffs, we have got police chiefs, we have got fire departments, we have the private sector, people that run flight schools in Florida, for example, that have got to be part of the information flow, both from the local level up, because they are really your largest set of eyes and ears about imminent threats.

Then, of course, the other way, you have to be able to share information. Along those lines, a lot of States have privacy protections that are, for example, in Florida, built into our Constitution. We have an explicit privacy clause.

So I would like, Mr. Marsh, as you talk about data mining, and also the Senator and the Congressman, to tell us what, if anything, as we decide whether or not to set up a privacy office in every single agency or every single sub-agency, whether we decide to put it at one major level of the Federal Government, whether that is inside the White House or whether that is independent—those debates are obviously ongoing. But I would like to have you tell us what we ought to focus on as we use the 280 million sets of eyes and ears around the country in sharing information up and down and how privacy can be adversely impacted if we are not careful in that flow of information stream as well.

Mr. HAMILTON. Mr. Feeney, I will try a cut at it, and I am sure others will want to contribute.

The first point I want to make is with regard to the link you suggest between intelligence and law enforcement. That is a very important link, and that is one of the reasons we didn't go to an MI-5, incidentally.

The fellow who is out here investigating a crime with the idea of prosecution in court will often pick up information that is very valuable to the intelligence side of the FBI, and vice versa. The person doing intelligence, looking at terrorist activity, often will pick up information that is very vital to the law enforcement side. So we think there is a natural synergy or link, if you would, between the two sides of the FBI.

The second point, we really did address quite frequently the need to push information down to the State and local officials. My recollection is somewhere in the report we say 18,000 local officials, police officials and others, are enormously important assets for us in terms of counterterrorism activity. And we did find, as I think maybe your question suggested, that that flow of information was not nearly as good as it ought to be. I think here, too, there have been improvements, incidentally, but there is a long way to go.

I believe I am correct in saying that a major concern of Director Mueller—I certainly don't want to try to speak for him—is to try to improve that flow of information to agents in the field; and in some cases, like New York City, I believe the relationship between the FBI and the New York City police is being worked out quite well.

But it is a huge advantage for us in counterterrorism to be able to take advantage of the local law enforcement people, and they simply must be brought into the information pool to a much greater extent than has been true in the past.

Now, the third point I am not sure I caught with regard to privacy. You wanted to know how it was adversely impacted by all of this?

Mr. FEENEY. Well, we have talked a lot about international privacy protections, sharing amongst Federal agencies. But as we go up and down from local, State and Federal and the other way, what do we need to think about in terms of protecting people's privacy there, too?

Mr. HAMILTON. It is a pervasive problem, because if you must, as we believe on the Commission, increase the flow of information, that means the privacy concerns are greater, and that is why we think there has to be some overall direction on it within the executive branch and a lot of review, as some of the other Members of the Committee have suggested, by courts and the Congress.

Mr. GORTON. Mr. Chairman, may I comment on Mr. Feeney's question?

Mr. CANNON. Absolutely. I think you will note I am fairly strict on the time frame for asking questions but try to allow some extension of that time, whereas we have not interrupted the answers which we find and I think the rest of the Committee finds fascinating. So, please, Mr. Gorton, go ahead.

Mr. GORTON. Mr. Feeney, I think you did have two separate questions. There has been a traditional and very legitimate objection on the part of local law enforcement officials all across the country that communications are one way, that the FBI wanted to get information from them, and rarely if ever shared it with them. Director Mueller has made significant attempts in this connection. The creation of a Joint Terrorism Task Force in every major FBI office in the country has done so.

Two weeks ago, I visited with the mayor of Seattle, the chief of police, and the fire chief and found that my city had done an excellent job in setting up and following some of our recommendations on emergency response, setting up the single command structure and the like, and asked him just that question. And the answer to that question was, yes, it is better, but it still has a long way to go. We are not getting all of the information down that we need, but progress has been made.

With respect to your other question on privacy, I think I might refer you to another report. I am a member of the Markle Foundation's study. In fact, with the permission of the Chairman, I am going to leave here in about 30 minutes. I am due at its meeting in Colorado this evening.

It has spent a tremendous amount of very constructive time on data mining, the questions that Mr. Scott asked, on what can be shared and how it ought to be shared and, very specifically on this sharing, how will we bring these thousands of local law enforcement agencies into this field with a very strong protection of human rights. It has now had two reports. Its second came out about 6 or 8 months ago. We referred to it in our opening testimony here, and I think it will be of great value to you in answering that question.

Mr. MARSH. Mr. Feeney, on the classification, you should be aware there are two systems to the classification in our country that involve national security and law enforcement. The national security is Confidential, Secret, Top Secret, Codeword. That is generally the result of an executive order over on the defense side. Clearance for those are extremely expensive, very hard to obtain. There is inability in our Government to transfer those from Department to Department, which is a major problem.

The second relates to the law enforcement type of issues that Senator Gorton spoke about. I served for 4½ years on the Gilmore Commission, which looked at local responders. The single most frequent complaint that we received from first responders from across the Nation was the failure to get sensitive or classified information to them that they needed for their security purposes. That has improved somewhat by a recent order of the Department of Homeland Security but not anywhere near where it needs to be.

This is another area, where some information comes down, and it is marked "law enforcement sensitive." Now, it is a form of classification. Very frequently, law officers with law enforcement sensitive information do not transfer that to other people who need to know it inside the community. You have broached a matter that is a major, major problem that is really administrative but has enormous impacts in other ways of operation.

Ms. O'CONNOR KELLY. Mr. Feeney, as the operational Privacy Officer on the panel, I note that a major focus of our work this past year has been addressing exactly the issue you have raised of information sharing both across the Federal Government but also with the State and local partners.

Obviously with the major homeland security efforts being undertaken at the State level, we are being forced to share—and we should be sharing—information with our State and local homeland security directors. I see it as sort of a four-tiered issue.

First of all, Homeland Security is made up of 22 different, separate parts of agencies. So we had to first construct a structure that allows information sharing within the Department, which was actually a major undertaking given the privacy act systems that existed in those agencies.

Then to share with other agencies—our partner agencies at both Defense and Justice and other parts of the Federal service to make those agencies more efficient in the use of information—then to share with our State and local partners. And finally to share with the private sector. With over 85 percent of our critical infrastructures in the hands of the private sector in this country, we have a need to share and a need to know information about their efforts.

And, of course, as has been pointed out, with the new rules under critical infrastructure sharing and sensitive homeland security information, we have hopefully heightened the ability to share, but also created good rules around the sharing that allows our employees to know what should be shared and what should not be shared, particularly when it pertains to individuals.

Mr. FEENEY. Thank you.

Mr. CANNON. I would like to thank the very thoughtful Vice Chairman of the Subcommittee for that thought-provoking inquiry.

And now the Chair recognizes the very patient Ranking Member of this Subcommittee for his opportunity to question for 5 minutes. Mr. Watt.

Mr. WATT. Thank you, Mr. Chairman.

And I think I will use my 5 minutes to follow up on some lines of questioning that other people have already opened before I go to one final overarching question that I would like to pose. First, Mr. Nadler raised an interesting question about if Congress can't get information from executive agencies, how we could set up a board or commission oversight board, and how they would get information to do the necessary job that we would give them.

It occurred to me that Ms. Kelly might be in a good position to respond to that. She is inside the Government, inside the executive branch.

How would we structure, you think, a board, oversight board, to do the kinds of things that the 9/11 Commission report has suggested, and give them the kind of authority and mechanisms to get the information that they need when we appear to be having trouble getting that kind of information ourselves? Can you share any light on that, either now or subsequent to the hearing?

If you have got some thoughts now, I would love to hear them.

Ms. O'CONNOR KELLY. Yes.

Mr. WATT. If you have follow-up thoughts I would love to hear them, too.

Ms. O'CONNOR KELLY. Well, I have certainly been thinking about this issue for many years, and people wiser than me have been thinking about it for many decades.

So I think there are a number of ways—and I don't want to preempt people in the Administration who may have thoughts on this themselves—but I think you hit on the exact point that the information on—perhaps it is human nature for people to not want to air their dirty laundry in public.

And so to have a privacy office within the Federal agency, although it is looked upon somewhat quizzically elsewhere in the world, has actually been a very effective structure because we are seen as a helpmate in the mission of the Department, but also someone who has criticized from within in advance of programs being launched. And perhaps that idea is being enacted.

But we also do rest heavily on our external role. And we have issued some critical reports of the Department, which we will be sharing with you in our annual report to Congress, which should be printed and finalized, hopefully, within a matter of weeks.

Mr. WATT. I take it that what the Commission has recommended goes beyond privacy officers or bodies within agencies.

Ms. O'CONNOR KELLY. Right.

Mr. WATT. You may be suggesting that each agency that is dealing in this arena needs a privacy officer. But what the Commission, I think, is suggesting is something that—that is——

Ms. O'CONNOR KELLY. Overseeing.

Mr. WATT.—kind of overseeing all of this. And it may be a more difficult problem to get agencies to give up the information to that external body than even to an internal body.

Ms. O'CONNOR KELLY. That may certainly be the case. And I think for that question, we should look to the experience of countries which already have operationalized independent data protection authorities. And there is ample evidence of their success, both in the European Union and also elsewhere in the world. It certainly might be worth even actually talking to some of those officials who lead those bodies.

There is an International Association of Data Protection individuals, which we participate in and represent the United States to the extent that we are welcomed in that body. They have met with greater and lesser success in their own countries in doing exactly what you have suggested, getting Federal agencies to share information about their operations, particularly when it might be damaging or embarrassing to the agency—but perhaps a very necessary process.

Mr. HAMILTON. Mr. Watt.

Mr. WATT. What I might suggest is ask—well.

Mr. HAMILTON. Mr. Watt, the key requirement——

Mr. WATT. I would just say one other thing that Ms. Kelly suggested, she maybe follow up with——

Ms. O'CONNOR KELLY. I would be happy to. Okay.

Mr. WATT.—some written suggestions in response to this, because I am going to run out of time. That is what I am worried about.

Mr. HAMILTON. Well, the key requirement is that Government agencies must be required to respond to the board. Now, the experience of the 9/11 Commission is that we had to have the subpoena power. We didn't use it very frequently. But if we had not had it, our job would have been much, much more difficult. And if this board is not able to require agencies to respond in detail to your questions, it will be ineffective.

Mr. WATT. Okay.

Mr. WATT. Mr. Chairman, I guess I am going to have to ask unanimous consent for a couple of extra minutes to get to the next two questions that I have.

Mr. CANNON. Without objection, so ordered.

Mr. WATT. Let me go. We used the whole 5 minutes on that one question.

I wanted to follow up on this national ID question that several people have kind of skirted around. The Commission's Report says—and I am quoting, I think—secure identification should begin in the United States. The Federal Government should set standards for the issuance of birth certificates and sources of identification such as driver's licenses. And then it goes on and says some other things.

Now, Representative Hamilton did a great job of telling us what he is not suggesting, which is a national ID. What I am a little unclear about, and what other people have raised a number of questions about, is what, short of a national ID, is the Commission suggesting here? Because it sounds like the only way you can get to where you are talking about is to have some kind of national identification system.

Mr. CANNON. If the gentleman would yield.

Could I just add to that, if you have Federal standards and a free-flow information system between the States and the Federal Government and law enforcement agencies and the Federal agencies, what is the difference between standards and a national ID?

Mr. GORTON. Very simply, everyone in the United States, or almost everyone in the United States, is comfortable with the idea that you have to have a driver's license in order to drive. Fifty states and all of the other jurisdictions issue driver's licenses. And they do so so that people can be identified, you know, when they are driving and when they are arrested.

What we are saying is that it is very important in the fight for the struggle for national security that people be able to be identified. We now have 50 or 54, whatever it is, different systems for that. And we are simply saying, take something that everyone accepts now and have it standardized in a way that it really identifies the people who are holding onto it. And we have also incidentally—and we have mentioned it in passing—that we ought to sort of have—it would be a great idea to have a standard form of birth certificates; because as one of the Members up here said, almost everything stems from that, you know, for Americans, all kinds of things you have to get a copy of your birth certificate for. And it ought to be something that is valid, that people can rely on.

We would like them to rely on driver's licenses. You don't have to get a driver's license if you don't want one. But if you want to drive, you do. Let's make it into—let's make it into something that really does say, when I pulled my driver's license out, you could be confident that this is really me and not somebody else.

Mr. CANNON. Would the gentleman yield?

Mr. WATT. Yes.

Mr. CANNON. What I hear you saying, Senator Gorton, is that you want a national ID, you want to get that through the back door by using something that everybody already accepts. But that is, I think you stated very clearly, that you want or you think the Commission wants the national ability to identify people and using an already accepted purpose. So if you want, if you want to drive in America, you have to be part of a federalized system of identification?

Mr. GORTON. I think there is a great deal of difference, Mr. Chairman, between something that you voluntarily go out and get and something that is mandated.

Mr. WATT. Well, you might—you might be—this might be a semantic discussion. And, I mean, I think the discussion about a national ID has been going back and forth for a number of years. But it does seem to me that if you are suggesting a standardized birth certificate, that is not optional. So for newly born individuals, that is a national ID; for people who obtain a driver's license, that is a national ID.

So you have left out people who have come into the United States who weren't born here and who don't get a birth certificate, or people who have opted not to get a driver's license. But you are not very far have having a requirement that you have some kind of national identification for those people, too, I would think.

Mr. HAMILTON. Well, I would——

Mr. GORTON. Mr. Watt, you have already got a national ID You have one or the other. You just don't know whether it is any good.

Mr. HAMILTON. Mr. Watt, just to let you know our concern here, all of these hijackers, except one, had U.S. Identification. And what we are saying is that secure identification is very, very important in terms of counterterrorism.

And we—we did not endorse a national ID. We think there is a distinction, as Senator Gorton has said, between Federal standards and having a national ID. But do not be deceived here with regard to the importance of identification. Keep in mind that these hijackers were extremely skillful in being able to find the gaps in our system. And we are trying to protect against that as best we can.

Mr. WATT. And do let me be clear that I am not either supporting or condemning a national identification system. All I am trying to do is figure out what—what those options are and be clear on what the Commission is suggesting. Because for us to move from the onset that you have expressed to the reality of what you have expressed requires our understanding what you had in mind. And that is all I am trying to do.

Let me do one other thing, Mr. Chairman. And I don't really think this question may be—well, anybody will want to answer—but I think I have got to ask it because there is, it appears to me, to be a real rush politically to act on the 9/11 Commission's Report and a real rush to—for security purposes to act on.

And I guess the thing that I am wrestling with here in light of all of the questions that have been raised in this hearing is how we can proceed responsibly to get to a real good product without giving the public the perception that we are somehow dragging our feet and being picky and not paying attention to details.

Did the Commission have any ideas about the timetable? I mean, obviously, we are 3 years beyond 9/11. Did the Commission have any ideas about the timetable for the implementation or passage of whatever legislative initiatives are required to implement the 9/11 Commission's recommendations?

Mr. GORTON. Most of the attention so far to our recommendations has been to those two, or several that have to do with the structure of our intelligence system, the national intelligence director, the national counterterrorism center. The former of those has been recommended by probably a dozen commissions over years.

I have got—one of our people yesterday had—no, no, meeting over in the Senate yesterday—he showed me a list of 48 commissions since 1947 that have talked about restructuring our intelligence agencies none of which was successful.

It came from here, you know. The joint—the Joint Intelligence Committees of the House and the Senate 2 years ago made a recommendation that is at least similar to that. Speaking for myself, I am inclined to hope that you do do something before the election in that respect.

Mr. WATT. Can we do something on that front without doing something on the fronts that we have been discussing here today?

Mr. GORTON. Well, certainly you can.

Mr. WATT. I mean, is it advisable? I know the answer is we can. The question is, would it be advisable to do something on that front without—without setting up these security measures for individual liberties and privacy that we all know need to be in place at the same time that the protections need to be in place.

Mr. GORTON. We believe that the recommendations that relate to the Committee, the subject of this Committee, are very, very important, Mr. Watt. We wouldn't have included them if we didn't. And we thought about them a great deal and dealt with them advisedly.

I guess the other side of that coin is simply this. We know those terrorist organizations are still out there. We know they have declared war against the United States of America. We know that, while either through good preparation or good fortune, in the almost 3 years since 9/11 no other terrorist attack has taken place in the United States. We also know that lots of them have taken place other places in the world.

So figuratively we have, if not literally, out there in the streets somewhere, is a bomb with a fuse and the fuse is lit. And we have no idea whether that fuse goes off in 5 days, 5 weeks, 5 months or 5 years. But it is going to be awfully hard to stop the blame game if it goes off when we have done nothing.

Mr. WATT. Thank you, Mr. Chairman. You have been very generous with your time. And I yield back.

Mr. CANNON. Thank you. I want to thank the Ranking Member for some very insightful questions.

I was not clear when we came into this hearing how clear you are from the Commission on the need for a national ID or a system of national identification. I think that has become very, very clear here.

In addition, I think the question about coming up with a good product versus looking like we are dragging our feet is a very insightful question. And my reaction to that is we need to do some things. I am appreciative of the Administration. I am thankful daily that we haven't had in America another serious terrorist activity.

Although I was doing a cottage meeting last night and had a very conservative person there who expressed, at some length and with some eloquence, appreciation for that, but recognized that we have terrorist groups in America that aren't associated with al Qaeda, groups that are doing things that by any definition are terrorist—and that includes some of our gang members, some of our ethnic gang members. We have some very serious problems to deal with. We have been very, very blessed. Al Qaeda or violent Islam is not our only problem. It is internal problems.

I just feel like we need to point out here—generally speaking, I almost never preach from the podium here, but often use this to ask questions. I was thinking about George Washington, since his name came up a couple of times. He was asked at one point what the purpose of the other body was. And he had cup of very hot coffee. And he took the cup and poured some in the saucer, swirled it around and then drank from the saucer. And he said, the People's House, Congress, the House of Representatives, is like a turbulent boiling, scalding cup of coffee. And the Senate, by the way this is before the 17th amendment—I am not sure it still holds—but the Senate is the area where we cool it down and sip.

I feel like we have barely sniffed the coffee, let alone gotten ready to cool it down or taste it here. So we have a very long way to go, but some things are really remarkable in our time.

In the first place, I look at Ms. O'Connor Kelly. We have had a long and very productive discussion. I think she has done a remarkably good job at what she has done. She represents private industry bringing the most current state-of-the-art understanding of technology into the Government. And Government is much better because of that.

And so as you are looking at the questions, Representative from Ohio—or Iowa, pardon me. As I am trying to go through these complex issues, my dear friend Mr. King suggested bureaucratization sets in. But Government is radically improved by the interface between free enterprise and new technology and our bureaucratic process.

But at the same time we are getting these little inputs that make DHS a much more successful agency, we are federalizing more and more issues. And we are doing it because it is easier to deal with many of the issues that face us today at a Federal level. And some of those are absolutely important to be federalized.

The State of Utah just recently passed a spyware bill. So my IT companies are thrilled with that bill. And I have to admit, the other day when I was talking to one of them, I said that I asked the governor to veto it. And the reason I asked her to veto it—obviously not very successfully—is because this is truly a Federal issue. You have to deal with that issue federally. And if you don't do it that way, you have chaos in our system. So we have this period of time where we are truly challenged. But the other side, we are responding to those challenges, sometimes appropriately, sometimes inappropriately with federalization of issues.

And I am just deeply concerned that in a time of conflict, that men of zeal without understanding, or people with zeal without understanding, are going to assert that we need to do things federally for which there is no alternative. There is theoretically another way to deal with that.

And, Mr. Marsh, you spoke twice about anonymizers. Now I think the original Web site that anonymized for people is actually in my district. Very cool. This goes way back—by the way—we are not claiming all the benefits of modern technology. But we have great opportunities with—with technology. And if we go down a path of federalization too quickly, we will end up with remarkable problems.

I cannot drive through my major city, Provo, Utah, my most central city, without being keenly aware that every stoplight has a camera. I am no computer wonk, but I know the process to be able to focus, with some artificial intelligence, the camera on the driver and get a picture of the driver, and on the license plate and get a picture of the license plate of every car that goes through every intersection that has a stoplight and a camera in that city.

That gives me the willies, and I think it gives Americans a bit of pause. On the one hand, a young woman who was kidnapped and the kidnapper was captured very quickly, in part by using some of this technology. We do want to stop kidnappers. We do want to stop terrorists.

But I just feel like here in this Subcommittee and in the Constitution Subcommittee as well, we need to be looking at these issues very carefully and drinking from that saucer and not scalding our tonsils as we chug the coffee immediately.

I also just feel the need to point out that what happened on 9/11 was tragic, and a great cost, but it was not entirely unanticipated. I think perhaps the magnitude of it was unanticipated. But when we set up the CIA and the FBI there was a debate, and that debate centered on the core principles that we have used to build all of our institutions in America, and that is separation of powers. And while, you know, as we look at that today, we need to be thinking in terms of the values incorporated and what was a system that didn't work very well and what we can do with technology today, which allows us to bridge the gap and still maintain separate centers of power, division of power.

If you read one of the most remarkable Founding Fathers, Thomas Jefferson, he spoke over and over and over again about taking power from the highest level of Government and shifting or keeping everything down at the lowest level. And if you fly over America today and you see the big squares; that is, the particular application of Thomas Jefferson's vision of how to organize society.

We did square townships so that towns could grow up in a context, and those townships could have smaller units all the way down to what we called wards, which were 100 families. And his idea of Government was that you govern at the 100-family level. And I believe the idea behind the concept of the well-organized militia for the second amendment, was that people in that 100-family unit would be able to assert police authority within that group.

Now, that is a concept that is embedded in our very geography in America, but which is not being considered, I don't think, today as we are looking at global attacks. And yet as I said earlier, all the attacks aren't global. Many of the attacks we have are home grown, homemade. They are not even foreign or different ethnicities from the bulk of the Northern Europeans who settled America. They are among us today, not appealing their sentences, because of the possibility of a death penalty if they get a new trial, or if he gets a new trial. So I am just—I am just deeply concerned about those things.

I wanted to touch on another couple of points that you made, Mr. Marsh.

You talked about a protocol or a culture of privacy. I remember thinking as a kid, no one, no employee of the IRS would ever give anyone information that the IRS collected. And then we had two Presidents, one of each party, who appear to have made even FBI raw data files available to people in the press. With that culture destroyed fundamentally—and that is not many people, if they have faith that their files are going to be kept private—we have to rebuild that culture somehow. Rebuilding that culture means going to people with technology at the lowest level where they can be protected and anonymizers are great possibilities. But you have other issues, like a certified identification, which hasn't been mentioned I don't think in any of these processes, which today is not used for anything but to avoid that little pop-up on your screen that says you are not a secure user. And you apparently can now pay $49 to get that pop-up eliminated. But it doesn't do anything for the issue of identification that we have been talking about here today.

And then finally, I just want to point out that there is a lot of vagueness in most Americans' thinking about what they want out of privacy. And so I would like to just pause at one of the problems, or weigh how to think about that.

If you saw the movie "Enemy of the State" with Will Smith, you have an innocent citizen who has something stashed in a bag that that then makes him the target of the vast bureaucracies of the CIA. And the appalling thing is the technology is all there. It was a very cool movie from that point of view.

The likelihood of any of us being the subject of a hunt by the CIA is almost nonexistent. But the premise of the film, if you will recall, is a Congressman of integrity who wouldn't vote in a certain way and therefore was murdered.

Now, I would like to think that all of my colleagues were men of, A, integrity and, B, they have never done anything they could be blackmailed with or that could be used to encourage them to vote a different way. But in most issues in America today, votes at the congressional level and the House of Representatives and the other body, or in city council, tend to be fairly narrow because we have hard choices. And the ability of evil men to get information on decisionmakers at any level of Government and thereby pervert decisions, that is what we are trying to avoid here.

And so while driving, I am not worried when my license plate is captured, my face is captured by a camera at an intersection. But cumulatively in America, we need to be concerned about that. Because if you can prove that a city councilman was at an intersection near the house of a woman he was purported to be having an affair with, there is something wrong with that. It's important to the large process of how we govern ourselves and how we get good men and women to perform public functions without the threat of embarrassment when an issue comes up that they need to exercise their judgment on.

Those are the areas at all levels of Government and in the judiciary as well, where I think the issues we are dealing with here are important and are worthy of being dealt with thoughtfully and carefully over time.

And I suspect that this Subcommittee, perhaps, the Constitution Subcommittee in addition, is going to have a lot to say about how we at least approach that problem. And I think that means a commission with people who are very thoughtful, who have significant background, and who are people who are willing to say we don't necessarily need to Federalize this process. And if we do Federalize this process, it shouldn't just be the damn Feds sucking information out of the local folks. It ought to be the local folks who get something back. And to do that you ought to have some kind of protection, maybe an anonymizer. It may be a culture that existed at one time in the Federal Government, I am not sure what it is. It is vital to America and it is, I think, the cornerstone of what our grandchildren are going to enjoy or suffer in the future.

So with that, are there any comments by anyone else on the panel or additional comments that you on the panel would like to make?

Thank you. I apologize for preaching, but we are adjourned.

[Whereupon, at 12:35 p.m., the Subcommittees were adjourned.]

# APPENDIX

## Material Submitted for the Hearing Record

Prepared Statement of the Honorable Chris Cannon, a Representative in Congress From the State of Utah, and Chairman, Subcommittee on Commercial and Administrative Law

The Subcommittees will please come to order.

Before we formally start today's proceedings, Chairman Chabot and I want to sincerely thank and recognize our colleagues on both Subcommittees and on both sides of the aisle for taking time out of their busy schedules to attend this important hearing. As many of you know, August is typically when Members of Congress return to their districts to catch up on constituent matters and spend time with their families. Unfortunately, in these extraordinary times, however, we must undertake extraordinary measures to deal with certain pressing issues.

It also goes without saying that we express our sincere gratitude to our esteemed witnesses, each of whom reflect the greatest hallmarks of public service. We appreciate your contributions to our deliberations today.

The title of today's hearing—Oversight Hearing on Privacy and Civil Liberties in the Hands of the Government Post-September 11, 2001: Recommendations of the 9/11 Commission and the U.S. Department of Defense Technology and Privacy Advisory Committee (which we'll refer to as "TAPAC")—clearly explains why we're here.

As many of you know, the 9/11 Commission filed its final report last month. As some of you may not know, however, is that the report includes several recommendations intended to protect our citizens' privacy and civil liberties. In addition, it recommends that the federal government set standards for the issuance of birth certificates and sources of identification, such as drivers' licenses, to promote secure identification information. While most media headlines have emphasized the Commission's anti-terrorism proposals, I believe the privacy and civil liberties recommendations are among those most critical to our nation's future and which will form part of the focus of our hearing.

Today's proceedings will also focus on certain recommendations that the TAPAC Committee made regarding safeguarding informational privacy. By way of background, TAPAC was established by Secretary Rumsfeld as an independent, bipartisan committee to examine the privacy ramifications presented by data mining activities by the Defense Department. I think we all agree that Secretary Rumsfeld is to be commended for taking this initiative and for ensuring that TAPAC's membership included some of our nation's most respected experts in the fields of constitutional and privacy law. I am informed that among the many luminaries who testified before TAPAC was our colleague from New York (Mr. Nadler).

Advances in technology have increasingly facilitated the collection and dissemination of personally identifiable information, but have also correspondingly increased the potential for misuse of such information. As the recently renamed Government Accountability Office observed, "These advances bring substantial federal information benefits as well as increasing responsibilities and concerns." Interestingly, TAPAC, over the course of its deliberations, determined that as the Defense Department was not alone in its conduct of data mining activities, it was necessary for it to address this issue through a series of Government-wide recommendations.

The purpose of today's hearing is to examine the validity of these recommendations and those of the 9/11 Commission that relate to privacy and civil liberties and to determine whether they warrant a legislative response. We would especially appreciate any guidance from our witnesses about how the Congress, in crafting legislation, can best protect our citizens' privacy without compromising legitimate law enforcement and terrorism detection efforts. And, as our witnesses know, it has been 30 years since a privacy commission was established as part of the Privacy Act of 1974. I would be interested in having our witnesses comment on whether now is the time to re-establish a privacy commission that would specifically focus on government privacy issues, especially given all the technological developments that have occurred since the commission filed its final report in 1977 and the current state of our nation's security concerns.

I should also note that both my Subcommittee—the Subcommittee on Commercial and Administrative Law—and Chairman Chabot's Subcommittee—the Constitution Subcommittee—have played a major role in with respect to protecting personal privacy and civil liberties in this era of heightened security under the leadership and guidance of Jim Sensenbrenner, the Chairman of the Judiciary Committee. As both the 9/11 Commission Report and TAPAC Report concluded, it is no easy task to balance the competing goals of keeping our nation secure and protecting the privacy rights of our nation's citizens. I believe that our respective Subcommittees and the Judiciary Committee are uniquely and best suited to study and resolve these issues.

Our accomplishments to date include the establishment of the first statutorily created privacy office in a federal agency, namely the Department of Homeland Security. We have also spearheaded the creation of a similar office in the Justice Department, which is contained in legislation now pending in the Senate. In addition, both my Subcommittee and the Constitution Subcommittee have considered and supported legislation requiring a federal agency to prepare a privacy impact analysis for proposed and final rules and to include this analysis in the notice for public comment issued in conjunction with the publication of such rules.

I will conclude my opening remarks with a quote from one of our founding fathers. As I think you'll agree, Mr. Hamilton's observations and warnings are as meaningful today as they were when he wrote them more than two hundred years ago:

"Safety from external danger is the most powerful director of national conduct. Even the ardent love of liberty will, after a time, give way to its dictates. The violent destruction of life and property incident to war, the continual effort and alarm attendant on a state of continual danger, will compel nations the most attached to liberty to resort for repose and security to institutions which have a tendency to destroy their civil and political rights. To be more safe, they at length become willing to run the risk of being less free."

---

## PREPARED STATEMENT OF THE HONORABLE STEVE CHABOT, A REPRESENTATIVE IN CONGRESS FROM THE STATE OF OHIO, AND CHAIRMAN, SUBCOMMITTEE ON THE CONSTITUTION

I'd like to thank Chairman Cannon for holding this important hearing today.

September 11, 2001, changed our world. It changed the way in which we view terrorism and the way in which we, as a country, must protect ourselves.

Since that tragic day, Congress acted quickly to protect the country from future terrorist attacks. For example, through the Patriot Act, we provided our law enforcement officials with enhanced investigative tools to prevent the planning of future attacks, and we authorized the creation of the Department of Homeland Security to better coordinate activities within our country to protect against the future threat of terrorism.

In taking action, we have been mindful of the protections afforded by our Constitution and our need to protect them as we protect our country. In the Patriot Act, we included protective measures, such as the sunset provisions. When authorizing the Department of Homeland Security, we ensured that a privacy officer position was established to examine the implications of the agency's rules and regulations on privacy and to address any issues that may result.

Over the last 20 months, the National Commission on Terrorist Attacks Upon the United States (9/11 Commission) has investigated the circumstances and events leading up to and on September 11.

In their report, the 9/11 Commission identified deficiencies within the federal government and made recommendations, including recommendations to safeguard privacy, to better protect the American public. While we must move expeditiously to make our country safer, we take care to do so in a thoughtful and Constitutional manner.

I look forward to discussing the Commission's recommendations with our witnesses today and determining what Congress can do to better protect the privacy of our citizens.

As we move forward, it is important to remember that having effective anti-terrorism measures does not necessarily comprise the protections afforded by our Constitution, as one is not the enemy of the other. The enemy is terrorism.

---

# Statement by Rep. Jerrold Nadler
# Hearing on the Recommendations of the 9/11 Commission and the DOD Technology and Privacy Advisory Committee
# August 20, 2004

Thank you, Mr. Chairman. Given the importance of this matter, and the fact that nearly three years have elapsed since the attacks of September 11, I am pleased that we have returned to consider the recommendations of the 9/11 Commission now, without waiting – as some have suggested – until next year.

Whatever conclusions members may ultimately draw about these recommendations, it is important that this work receive our immediate and careful consideration.

I want to welcome our former colleagues, Rep. Hamilton, and Sen. Gorton, and to thank them for the important work they and their colleagues have done.

I am also pleased that we have Secretary Marsh here today. The issues that gave rise to the Secretary's Technology and Privacy Advisory Committee are also implicated in the Commission's recommendations, so it is important that we have the benefit of your work.

Finally, I want to welcome back Ms. O'Connor Kelly. The 9-11 Commission has recommended, in somewhat general terms, that we set up a Civil Liberties Oversight Board. The TAPAC Commission has similarly recommended that the Secretary of Defense create a "policy-level privacy officer." Congress will have to work out the details. I hope that your experience as the Privacy Officer for the Department of Homeland Security can shed some light on how we might ensure the independence and effectiveness of the offices created pursuant to these recommendations.

The need to improve capabilities and coordination within the intelligence and law enforcement communities was all too well demonstrated on Sept. 11. Thousands of innocent citizens, who did nothing more that board an aircraft or go to work, were barbarically slaughtered. We ignore, at our nation's peril, the lessons we can draw from the intelligence failures leading up to those crimes, and from other recent intelligence fiascos.

At the same time, increased governmental powers carry with them increased risks to the rights of all citizens. We expect our government to keep us safe, but we are also a nation with a healthy mistrust of unfettered governmental power. Our whole system of government combines limited powers, with checks and balances, that must be maintained. Rights sacrificed in a time of emergency are often lost forever; actions taken in the heat of the moment are often a source of shame and regret to later generations.

So our job is to strike an appropriate – and workable – balance. That is not easy. As the members of the Commission have noted:

Many of our recommendations call for the government to increase its presence in our lives .... Therefore, while protecting our homeland, Americans should be mindful of threats to vital personal and civil liberties. This balancing is no easy task, but we must constantly strive to keep it right. This shift of power and authority to the government calls for an enhanced system of checks and balances to protect the precious liberties that are vital to our way of life. [Report pp 393-394].

Similarly, the TAPAC Commission noted:

We believe it is possible to use information technologies to protect national security without compromising the privacy of U.S. persons. The answer lies in clear rules and policy guidance, adopted through an open and credible political process, supplemented with educational and technological tools, developed as an integral part of the technologies that threaten privacy, and enforced through appropriate managerial, political, and judicial oversight. [p x]

With that sound guidance in mind, I welcome our panel and look forward to your testimony.

Thank you, Mr. Chairman.

APEX
TP
*9780160742323*
76901953 – 76

# REPORT FROM THE FRONT LINE: FORT WAYNE'S BATTLE AGAINST DRUGS

## HEARING

BEFORE THE

SUBCOMMITTEE ON NATIONAL SECURITY, INTERNATIONAL AFFAIRS, AND CRIMINAL JUSTICE

OF THE

COMMITTEE ON GOVERNMENT REFORM AND OVERSIGHT
HOUSE OF REPRESENTATIVES

ONE HUNDRED FOURTH CONGRESS

SECOND SESSION

JUNE 24, 1996

Printed for the use of the Committee on Government Reform and Oversight

U.S. GOVERNMENT PRINTING OFFICE

43–353 CC WASHINGTON : 1997

For sale by the U.S. Government Printing Office
Superintendent of Documents, Congressional Sales Office, Washington, DC 20402
ISBN 0-16-055739-9

## COMMITTEE ON GOVERNMENT REFORM AND OVERSIGHT

WILLIAM F. CLINGER, JR., Pennsylvania, *Chairman*

BENJAMIN A. GILMAN, New York
DAN BURTON, Indiana
J. DENNIS HASTERT, Illinois
CONSTANCE A. MORELLA, Maryland
CHRISTOPHER SHAYS, Connecticut
STEVEN SCHIFF, New Mexico
ILEANA ROS-LEHTINEN, Florida
WILLIAM H. ZELIFF, JR., New Hampshire
JOHN M. McHUGH, New York
STEPHEN HORN, California
JOHN L. MICA, Florida
PETER BLUTE, Massachusetts
THOMAS M. DAVIS, Virginia
DAVID M. McINTOSH, Indiana
JON D. FOX, Pennsylvania
RANDY TATE, Washington
DICK CHRYSLER, Michigan
GIL GUTKNECHT, Minnesota
MARK E. SOUDER, Indiana
WILLIAM J. MARTINI, New Jersey
JOE SCARBOROUGH, Florida
JOHN B. SHADEGG, Arizona
MICHAEL PATRICK FLANAGAN, Illinois
CHARLES F. BASS, New Hampshire
STEVEN C. LaTOURETTE, Ohio
MARSHALL "MARK" SANFORD, South Carolina
ROBERT L. EHRLICH, JR., Maryland

CARDISS COLLINS, Illinois
HENRY A. WAXMAN, California
TOM LANTOS, California
ROBERT E. WISE, JR., West Virginia
MAJOR R. OWENS, New York
EDOLPHUS TOWNS, New York
JOHN M. SPRATT, JR., South Carolina
LOUISE McINTOSH SLAUGHTER, New York
PAUL E. KANJORSKI, Pennsylvania
GARY A. CONDIT, California
COLLIN C. PETERSON, Minnesota
KAREN L. THURMAN, Florida
CAROLYN B. MALONEY, New York
THOMAS M. BARRETT, Wisconsin
BARBARA-ROSE COLLINS, Michigan
ELEANOR HOLMES NORTON, District of Columbia
JAMES P. MORAN, Virginia
GENE GREEN, Texas
CARRIE P. MEEK, Florida
CHAKA FATTAH, Pennsylvania
BILL BREWSTER, Oklahoma
TIM HOLDEN, Pennsylvania
ELIJAH CUMMINGS, Maryland

---

BERNARD SANDERS, Vermont (Independent)

JAMES L. CLARKE, *Staff Director*
KEVIN SABO, *General Counsel*
JUDITH McCOY, *Chief Clerk*
BUD MYERS, *Minority Staff Director*

---

### SUBCOMMITTEE ON NATIONAL SECURITY, INTERNATIONAL AFFAIRS, AND CRIMINAL JUSTICE

WILLIAM H. ZELIFF, JR., New Hampshire, *Chairman*

ROBERT L. EHRLICH, JR., Maryland
STEVEN SCHIFF, New Mexico
ILEANA ROS-LEHTINEN, Florida
JOHN L. MICA, Florida
PETER BLUTE, Massachusetts
MARK E. SOUDER, Indiana
JOHN B. SHADEGG, Arizona

KAREN L. THURMAN, Florida
ROBERT E. WISE, JR., West Virginia
TOM LANTOS, California
LOUISE McINTOSH SLAUGHTER, New York
GARY A. CONDIT, California
BILL BREWSTER, Oklahoma
ELIJAH CUMMINGS, Maryland

EX OFFICIO

WILLIAM F. CLINGER, JR., Pennsylvania
CARDISS COLLINS, Illinois

ROBERT CHARLES, *Staff Director and Chief Counsel*
SEAN LITTLEFIELD, *Professional Staff Member*
IANTHE SAYLOR, *Clerk*
CHERRI BRANSON, *Minority Professional Staff Member*